PARIS FOR LIFE

Paris for Life

Notes from a Lifetime in and out of Paris

Barry Frangipane

ISBN   978-0-9836141-4-2   (Hardcover)
          978-0-9836141-3-5   (Paperback)
          978-0-9836141-5-9   (Ebook)

Library of Congress Control Number 2023915296

Savory Adventures Publishing
Orlando, Florida

First Printing, 2024

Editor: Red Adept Editing
Layout: From Manuscript to Book
Cover Photo: Stefano Zanarello © 2023

This is a work of nonfiction. Names, characters, places, and incidents however are either products of the author's fallible memory or have been changed to protect the privacy of individuals.

Dedication

To Heidi, who taught me so much about France and about life; to my parents, who allowed me at twenty-one to follow my dreams in Paris and beyond; to my wife, Dolce Debbie, who has made our quarter century together even brighter than the City of Light; and of course, to Paris, which embraced me, teased me, and helped me learn life's most important lessons. Yes, Ernest, you were correct. Paris is a moveable feast, for which my hunger is still insatiable. — BF

Contents

Foreword..ix

First Date... 1
The Invite...25
Living Together...37
A Student in Paris...51
Working in Paris 75
Dreams Change 115
The Occasional Visitor 129
The Frequent Guest... 151
Déjà Vu... 187
Freedom 193
Paris for Life.. 219
Epilogue 225

Bibliography... 229
Useful Addresses... 231
About the Author... 233

Foreword

It is my pleasure to introduce you to *Paris for Life*, written by my dear friend Barry Frangipane. As a trilingual world traveler, storyteller, and author, Barry has the gift of transporting you to the heart of Paris with his vivid descriptions and witty humor. He has a unique talent for describing even the simplest pleasures of life, such as a baguette-and-cheese plate, in a way that will leave you salivating and dreaming of your next trip to the city of love.

I first met Barry at a dinner party where all the guests were strangers. Throughout the night, I got to know him and was struck by his unique perspective on life and his adventures. Barry's stories and experiences were captivating and left me feeling inspired to see the world through his eyes. I also had the pleasure of meeting his wife, Dolce Debbie, a larger-than-life chef who exudes beauty both inside and out. Together, they make a remarkable couple and are a true inspiration to all those who meet them. They are the friends everyone wants to have, and I am so lucky to adopt them as part of my family. Meeting Barry and Debbie that night was a life-changing experience for me, and I could fill a book with all the ways they've impacted my life, from our unforgettable trips to Europe to the kind gesture of picking up a friend at the airport, a man who is now my husband.

Paris for Life is not just a travel guide; it is a love letter to the city of Paris and a celebration of life's simple pleasures. Whether you are a seasoned traveler or dreaming of your first trip abroad, this book is a must-read. So sit back, pour yourself a glass of wine, and let Barry take you on a journey that will leave you enchanted and inspired.

— April Simpson, Executive Producer
Producergirl Productions

First Date

Over a thousand people took my picture during my first hour in Paris. They came by the busload, excited to take a photo, then returned quickly to their buses. Even as I stood on one leg while making faces, their shutters continued to snap.

As I waited for more than an hour for my friend Heidi to show up, I imagined each of these tourists upon returning from their vacation in France, showing off their photos of Notre Dame. They would notice me standing at the base of the Gothic arch outside the front entrance, eyes crossed and tongue sticking out, forever photobombing their travel memories.

Notre Dame Cathedral is a curious structure. The roof was made from thirteenth-century oak, coated with lead to prevent leaks. Towering over the cathedral is a steeple from

Notre Dame Cathedral

the 1800s surrounded by statues of the twelve apostles looking up at the commanding wooden spire. Since it opened in 1345, Notre Dame's gargoyles have struck fear into the hearts of both men and women. On sunny days, the figures look down from above with disapproving stares. But on stormy days, doubling as rain spouts, they resemble medieval creatures hung over from a night on the town, retching water on the townsfolk below.

The cathedral still stands only because German general Dietrich von Choltitz in August 1944 refused to obey Hitler's order to burn it down. And on the bright day I was there in January 1979, the structure basked in the winter sun while a steady stream of tourists photographed one of the most sacred cathedrals in Christianity.

With suitcases safely stored at the train station, I awaited my friend Heidi. This would be my first night in the apartment she had picked out for us in a residential neighborhood of Paris. I was pondering how I'd wound up standing in front of Notre Dame when the cathedral's bells rang twelve times and Heidi arrived.

WE MET BY CHANCE - 1976

In 1976, I worked as a foreign exchange teller at United Bank of Boulder while attending the University of Colorado. Customers purchased francs, lire, pounds, and Australian dollars, excited as they described their upcoming trips. Upon returning, they would turn in their currency and show me photos of their adventures. At eighteen, I was a Florida boy who had never made it any farther than Colorado and was beginning to dream of all the places "out there" just waiting for me to experience them.

"I need your help." The bank manager explained her situation as I was counting my various currencies at the end of the day. "As part of a banking exchange program, a banker from the Swiss Bank Corporation in Zurich will be here for two months to learn about the American banking system. We would like her to work side by side with you and for you to teach her everything you know."

Heidi Stettler arrived the following week. At five foot four with straight black hair reaching halfway down her back, she was nothing like the Swiss girl I had imagined. She spoke German, French, Italian, Romansh, Tagalog, Mandarin, and English. The only child of a Swiss father and a Philippine mother, this twenty-three-year-old was well-traveled.

Over the next few months, Heidi learned about American banks, including odd innovations such as our twenty-four-hour drive-through lanes and tellers on roller skates. Meanwhile, she talked about life in Switzerland and helped me try to remember my beginner's French from high school. Although she spoke perfect English, she would feign a lack of comprehension, forcing me to attempt to speak in French. I was intrigued by how much she knew about banking and about other countries. But since she was so much older than me, it was probably normal for her to know that much. Unfortunately, with my work schedule and university classes, I had no opportunity to get to know this Heidi Stettler outside of the bank.

By the time she returned to Switzerland, I was desperate to travel. There were so many places I wanted to see—France, Italy, Switzerland—and the list grew rapidly. Her last comment to me before she departed was "If you ever get to Europe, let me know, and I'll show you around Switzerland."

FIRST LOVE - 1977

"It's true, you never forget your first love. And for me,
that will always be Paris." — Caitriona Balfe, actor

———— ◆ ————

Mom was nine years old when she came to the United States
in the fall of 1937. She left northern Italy as tensions were
rising in that region of the world, and her family was happy
to start a new life in America. Forty years had passed, and
she had never returned to Italy to visit relatives in her home
country.

After I left the University of Colorado and returned to
my parents' home in Florida, I had very few expenses. I
found a job as a computer programmer at Milton Roy Corporation in St. Petersburg. It was time, I thought, to make
my mother an offer.

"Mom, I'm making a decent salary and saving quite a bit
by living at home. What would you say if I took you back
to Italy on vacation, with a stop in Paris?"

She was ecstatic. By the end of October, I had saved
enough money for my mother, father, and me to head to
Europe for three weeks. My mom and I were as excited as
little children, forever with the map on the kitchen table,
again and again planning our trip. We would spend a few
days in Paris, then I would head to Switzerland to meet up
with Heidi while Mom and Dad flew to Italy. I would catch
up with them in my mother's hometown of Treviso before

First Date

we returned to Paris together for our flight home. Finally, in the spring of 1977, we left for Paris, the first stop on our family vacation and my first travel out of the country.

The Metro whisked us from the airport to the underground Luxembourg station in the heart of the Latin Quarter. I ran up the escalator, through the turnstile, past a photo booth, and out the door. There she was—Paris. With Boulevard Saint-Michel at my feet and Luxembourg Gardens straight ahead, Paris welcomed me. Moreover, I felt like she was welcoming me back after a very long absence. The air had a dreamy scent, like that of a shirt left behind by a lover, reminding me of times past. I closed my eyes and inhaled. I was overcome with a sensation I had never experienced before, that of truly being home. And not the usual home but a place where someone had spent a past life and was now returning.

I hardly noticed my parents, who had followed me. My father gazed at a small kiosk located outside a jazz bar called Le Petit Journal. The kiosk was no more than four feet wide, with a green awning and the word *Crepes* in large letters. A middle-aged man with short dark hair and a weathered face greeted us.

"Bonjour, mes amis. Crepe?" His menu had crepes of every variety—sweet, buckwheat, banana-chocolate, chocolate-and-Grand-Marnier, butter-sugar, egg-and-cheese, ham-and-egg, and even a Greek crepe with feta cheese and oregano.

As the vendor made my egg-and-cheese crepe, he sprinkled oregano liberally over the cheese, saying in

Crepe kiosk outside Luxembourg Metro station

broken English, "Oregano—good for you!" My father's ham-and-egg crepe also received a good dose of oregano. Only my mother escaped this oregano exuberance since hers was made with banana and chocolate.

With a crepe of French perfection in hand, I instinctively led my parents to our hotel on Rue des Écoles.

"But how do you know where you're going?" my mother asked.

"I just know. It's down the hill and to the right."

The Hôtel Saint-Jacques had a small unassuming lobby with a wooden key rack within reach for guests. The young man behind the counter politely struggled to understand my French, but after I showed him our passports, he checked us in. Our room key had a fob the size of a baseball attached, and a sign stated in English, "Please do not take the room keys when you leave the hotel property. Please place them back the rack." This was a simple system to eliminate lost keys, and the fob ensured no one would leave with the key in their pocket.

The desk clerk mentioned something about the shower and asked if we needed coins, but I had trouble understanding him. Why, I wondered, would we need coins in our hotel room?

The three of us attempted to get into the elevator together, but it could fit a maximum of only one person and one small piece of luggage. We devised a plan. Dad went up alone without luggage to the fourth floor. He sent the elevator down empty, and we sent our pieces of luggage up to him one by one. When my mother finally boarded the elevator, I ran up three flights of stairs to the fourth floor, or so I thought. It turns out that in Europe, the lobby is on the ground floor, and the first floor is up a flight of stairs. So the fourth floor in France would be called the fifth floor in the USA. Lesson learned.

I climbed one more flight of stairs and caught up with my parents in the room. Mom was perplexed.

"But where is the toilet?" she asked.

I had forgotten to mention that we would share bathroom facilities with other guests. "Oh, it's down the hall, next to the showers, on the other side of the elevator. Only a few of the rooms had private baths, and they were considerably more expensive than rooms like ours."

"After that long flight, I'm ready for a nice long shower," Dad announced.

He shuffled to the bathroom with his fuzzy blue slippers from home and the tiny towel provided by the hotel.

He returned once, having forgotten his change of clothes, and once more for the shampoo.

"For Christ's sake, Louis, what did you forget this time?" Mom asked when he returned the third time.

"The shower is coin-operated! Does anyone have twenty centimes?"

I supplied my father with the requisite change, and off he went again.

When he returned, he was shivering and still had quite a bit of soap in his hair. In fact, he had more soap than hair. "The twenty cents bought me five minutes of hot water, then it started coming out freezing cold, so I quickly shut it off and got out!"

Mom dried off his soapy hair, and I made a note to get more coins for the morning. But for the time being, I would leave my parents to relax in the room.

I had a date with Luxembourg Gardens.

LUXEMBOURG GARDENS - 1977

Armed with a pen and drawing pad, I strolled down Boulevard Saint-Michel and straight to Luxembourg

Gardens. The park was surrounded by an iron fence painted in dark green with gold arrowheads atop each post. Elm trees lined the perimeter and blanketed the walkways with shade, like a protective mother holding an umbrella over her child in the bright sun.

A wide-open space led to a semicircular stairway and down to a large pond with a fountain of water shooting up from the center. Across the surface of the pond were numerous model sailboats. The boats were almost as large as the children standing on the edge of the pond with long white sticks, which they used to guide their crafts across the waters.

Hundreds of heavy green metal chairs were occupied by couples, elderly and young, interested solely in each other. Some read, others wrote, and many conversed in languages I couldn't even identify let alone understand. In a few chairs, artists drew in charcoal or pencil on sketch pads like the one in my hand. Most sketched the pond or the Senate building just beyond. I pulled up a chair, positioned it to be caressed by the sunlight between the trees, and opened my sketch pad.

John Ruskin, a writer of the 1850s, believed that "the sight is a more important thing than the drawing." He explained, "I would rather teach drawing that my pupils may learn to love nature, than teach the looking at nature that they may learn to draw." This quote had inspired me to push beyond my stick figure repertoire and attempt to draw a pond and a Senate building.

For thirty minutes, I basked in the sun with my pad open, with no ink applied to the paper. After an hour, there was still nothing on my pad. But for the first time, I had noticed other things around me. Bordering the large patches of grass in the park were hundreds of vibrant flowers, some yellow, some violet. They were probably pansies, each seemingly hand-painted with a face on the petals. As the breeze blew, these faces seemed to look left then right, keeping close track of the visitors to their garden.

Larger-than-life statues surrounded the landscape every few yards as if they were watching over me. Behind the statues of queens and princesses of days gone by, children laughed. Dressed in a blue or red chemise or even a frilly pink dress, they rode ponies in the park. Nearby, a couple shared both a chair and a sandwich, made from what appeared to be ham on a demi-baguette with either cheese or butter oozing out the sides.

I paid closer attention to the sailboats on the pond. Each had two sails in bright colors—yellow, blue, red, or green. The children cheered on their ships, probably imagining themselves in a real regatta. Almost inconsequential in this idyllic setting, the Eiffel Tower sat in the distance. The iron structure was austere in comparison to the sounds and colors surrounding me.

Trying again to draw, I made it as far as a poor sketch of the clock on the Senate building. But how could I draw the sounds of the laughter and the perfume of the flowers? How could I depict the feeling of living history in this park

First Date

created in 1612 by Marie de Medici, an Italian who became the queen of France?

I closed my pad, then my eyes, and just listened. John Ruskin had played a trick on me. He had never intended for me to draw. He intended for me to see. After returning to the hotel, I possessed the most complete depiction of the park—all recorded in my mind. Years later, I would still be able to relive the smells, the sounds, and the feeling of my first visit to Luxembourg Gardens.

The next morning, after enjoying a nice hot forty-centime shower, I said goodbye to my parents for a while and boarded a train to Zurich to meet with Heidi.

ZURICH - 1977

The early-morning sunlight enhanced the shimmering of the leaves on the trees as the train left Gare de Lyon and headed toward Zurich. Staring out of my train-car window, I watched Paris fade into the distant haze. We had met only yesterday, and I was already leaving. It was a bittersweet feeling, rather like receiving a gift then having it taken away. Before I finished my café au lait and the last crumbs of my croissant, vineyards dotted the landscape, interspersed with small towns. Every town seemed to have its own clock tower and castle.

As the train traversed the snow-capped Alps and slowly wound around the hills, it hit me—I didn't know German. In a few hours, the train would stop at the Zurich train station, and Heidi would be waiting for me on the platform. Or not. What if she wasn't there? On my second day ever outside the United States, I was heading to a German-speaking city to see Heidi, a meeting I'd confirmed in a letter a month earlier. If she didn't show up, I would have no idea how to say:

"Please. Thank you."

"Where is the restroom?"

"I need a train ticket back to Paris."

"Do you take French francs?"

"I'm hungry."

"This was a dumb idea."

"I love Swiss chocolate. Now, can you help me get home?"

The train pulled into the station in Zurich as unintelligible announcements were made in German over the public address system. To my relief, a girl with short black hair and a dark complexion, wearing a white T-shirt, denim skirt, and sandals, was waiting for me outside the train. The sight of my friend smiling and waving was reassuring. Heidi had recently cut her hair and was dressed much more casually than she had been at the bank in Colorado when I last saw her. As we left the platform, she filled me in on her latest news. While happy to see Heidi, I looked over my shoulder at the train. I missed Paris already.

Heidi's bright-red two-door Innocenti Mini had barely enough room for two fully grown humans, let alone luggage. Thankfully, I had only one small suitcase. But I imagined the car probably went far on a tank of gas. We sped down the autobahn in the tiny red bullet.

"So, how did you like Paris?" Heidi asked.

I had barely begun to respond when the engine started sputtering. She took the next exit, and the car coasted into a gas station.

"That's odd. The gas light only came on yesterday, and we're already out of gas."

"Heidi, this station is closed. There's no one here."

"Don't worry. They have coin-operated gas pumps. Here. Put this one-franc coin into the slot."

But the slot was jammed, possibly with another coin. We pushed the car to the other pump. It, too, was jammed.

"Looks like we'll have to fix it ourselves," Heidi said.

She unscrewed the cover of the gas pump with her Swiss Army knife. The inside of the pump was a maze of tubes, wires, and a thin metal channel directing the coins to the nearly full money box deep inside the assembly. The police would undoubtedly arrive any second, and I would spend the rest of my life in a Swiss jail, never to see my family again while drowning my sorrows in a daily ration of Swiss chocolate. Regrettably, one other German expression I had failed to learn before arriving was "Honest, Officer, I came here all the way from the United States to fix this gas pump, using only a Swiss Army knife, which, by the way, your country does a great job making."

When Heidi stuck her hand into the pump, the entire coin system collapsed with a *ding, ding, ding,* but we managed to get one liter of gas into her car. She didn't feel it necessary to reassemble the pump before we sped off for a week of touring Switzerland in her tiny car. During those seven days, I got to know Heidi better than I had during our entire time working together in Colorado. We played hide-and-seek in Château de Chillon, soaked each other with water at Rhine Falls, and skied in Verbier. Heidi was a smart girl with a keen sense of humor. We could be great friends, I thought, if we lived in the same country.

Barry Frangipane in Switzerland, 1977

LIFE CHANGES

At the week's end, my yearning for cheese, potatoes, and bread had been satisfied. Heidi took me to the train station, where we hugged and promised to visit each other again.

After saying goodbye, I took the train from Zurich to Treviso to catch up with my parents in Mom's hometown.

I spoke no Italian, but my mother had given me written instructions. "Get off the train, exit the station, and get on the Number 10 bus, giving the bus driver two fifty-lire coins for a bus ticket. Make sure you have two fifty-lire coins, because the ticket machine on the bus only accepts exact change." I was to get off the bus at Via Bibano, where I would recognize her aunt's house from the photograph in my pocket.

It was raining when I arrived at the Treviso train station. I remembered that I would need coins and stopped at the newsstand to get the required change.

The young lady was packing up for the night as I hurriedly gave her a five-hundred-lire note to purchase a newspaper. She gave me a couple of two-hundred-lire notes in return. Still, I had no change. I held up a pack of gum and handed her one of the two-hundred-lire notes. She took the money and counted back five pieces of candy as change. She locked the register drawer and stepped out from behind the counter.

"Ciao," she said then waved goodbye.

My heart sank.

Clearly, the candy was not going to get me on the bus. Ready to cry, I walked outside and sat in the rain on the steps in front of the train station. Roughly two miles from my parents, I couldn't get on the bus.

A tiny white car with the word *Taxi* on the side pulled alongside the curb at the bottom of the steps. The man in the driver's seat leaned over and stared at me through the passenger window. Unsure how to ask for help in Italian but realizing this could be my only chance, I pulled the photo of my relatives' house from my pocket.

"Via Bibano!" I said tentatively, displaying the picture of my intended destination.

The driver leaned over and opened the passenger door. Without another word, we were off. He seemed to know exactly where he was going. Thirty minutes and nine thousand lire later, I was reunited with my parents and introduced to Italian aunts and uncles.

Mom gave me a towel to dry off with as I explained about taking the taxi instead of the bus. She relayed my story to Zio Meno, her uncle, a gregarious man who laughed heartily then led me into his room and opened the top drawer of a large dresser. It was full of coins! He explained something in Italian to my mother before bursting into laughter once again.

"There's a coin shortage in Italy," she translated. "Everyone is holding onto them so they don't run out!"

Zio Meno clapped his hand on my shoulder and advised me not to worry about finding change for the bus. "This is Italy. No one pays anyway," he assured me with a chuckle.

The aunts nodded.

After dinner that night, my mother translated as Zio Meno introduced me to grappa, the local moonshine, and we toasted my first lesson in Italian economics and culture.

Still, I couldn't stop thinking about Paris. After we spent a few days with my mother's relatives, Mom and Dad flew back to Paris. I chose to take the night train from Venice, and it would arrive at Gare de Lyon the following morning. Each room in my second-class car had six couchettes, or bunk beds, three on each side. I took the middle bunk while a girl about my age took the top bunk. My view of the countryside through the night was partially obstructed by her long brown hair hanging over the side of the couchette above. I felt a bit uncomfortable, like I was somewhere I shouldn't be.

Returning from the restaurant car in the morning, I found the couchettes had been folded up into the wall, and my roommate sat by the window with tears in her eyes, staring outside as we approached Paris. The fog from the farmland had dissipated, and the sun peeked from behind the buildings.

We were only a few minutes from Gare de Lyon when she said, "This is my first trip out of Iran. I feel so over-whelmed, so free. How will I ever go home after a month here?"

I couldn't imagine the emotions she was feeling, being able to go and do as she pleased—and wear what she pleased—for the first time in her life.

We sat together staring out the window, hardly noticing the other travelers in our room as they prepared their belongings. Leaving the train station, we went in different directions. She was headed for a life-changing month while I was going to Hôtel Saint-Jacques to rejoin my parents.

Mom and Dad were planning their day to include a restaurant recommended by the hotel desk clerk.

Gare de Lyon

"Do you remember the young man you were struggling to communicate in French with last week?" my mom asked. "He speaks perfect English! He told us about a blue-collar restaurant near Metro Richelieu-Drouot called Le Bouillon Chartier, which has been open since the late 1800s. Put your bags down and come with us."

It was a bustling two-story restaurant with the clientele mostly consisting of workers in blue jumpsuits, and retirees. Dad held up three fingers, and the waiter in a white shirt and black vest sat us at a table overlooking the street below. Already seated at our table for four was an elderly Frenchman, halfway through his wine and boeuf bourguignon. Mom, Dad, and I had each ordered a glass of red wine when our tablemate spoke to the waiter.

"No. A carafe of red for the three of them." By writing on the paper tablecloth, he explained to us how one full carafe was cheaper than three individual glasses. By

pointing at his plate and nodding vigorously, he recommended ordering the stew.

While enjoying my boeuf bourguignon, I noticed a wall
full of tiny drawers, each with a number on the front. Our
waiter, who spoke a little English, unlocked the mystery of
the drawers. In days past, each regular customer had a
drawer in which they would store their cloth napkin for
reuse during the week. At the end of the week, the patrons
took the napkins home to wash them before returning them
the following Monday. As the waiter was explaining the
history of the drawers, he apparently noticed that the
couple at the next table had left. Midsentence, he refilled
our bread basket by combining their uneaten slices with
ours. I suddenly lost my appetite for bread.

When Dad asked for the check, the waiter wrote on the
tablecloth the name of each dish we'd ordered and circled
the total amount of the bill.

As we walked to the hotel, contemplating our departure
the next day, a thin veil of rain fell over the city. Although
the curtain was closing on our trip, something inside me
had changed. I had fallen in love with Paris and silently
planned my next visit to see her again.

SUMMER 1977

August was sweltering hot when I returned to Paris. She
was full of tourists, but the Parisians were gone. As the
local news vendor explained, most of the large businesses

shut down in August, and everyone heads to the beach. Since most of the workers are gone for the entire month, the bakeries and butchers also close.

"But where do those of us still in town buy bread?" I asked.

The news vendor explained. "Since the 1700s, there has been a law that at least one bakery in each of the twenty arrondissements must stay open in August. We can't be without our croissants and baguettes, you know."

The man who'd made my crepe back in May was still on the job in August, outside the Luxembourg Metro station as before. "Beurre-sucre," I said, ordering a butter-sugar crepe.

"Where are your mother and father?" he asked in broken English.

I explained that they couldn't make this particular trip.

In addition to my butter-sugar crepe, he handed me another one with egg, cheese, and oregano. "Eat this one for your mother."

Hands full with two crepes, I wandered into Luxembourg Gardens in search of shade and a respite from the smell of exhaust fumes in the summer air.

While walking the gardens built by Queen Marie de Médicis, I came upon a basin roughly one hundred feet long populated by large orange and white fish. It was shaded by tall elms, lined with flowerpots, and isolated from the rest of the park by winding vines in full bloom. At the end of the basin was a fountain with a statue of two lovers undressed and completely absorbed in each other and a jilted lover looking down on them from above. The sign read, "The Medici Fountain: Polyphemus surprising Acis and Galatea." I couldn't be sure, but it looked like Acis and Galatea were about to be in a whole lot of trouble.

Medici Fountain, Luxembourg Gardens

Sitting in the shade alongside the fountain, I found that the rest of Paris disappeared. There were no sounds of cars, buses, no voices, just the serenity of the light flickering off the surface of the water, the bright orange of the flowers in the pots, and the statue of Acis and Galatea, completely unaware of their impending doom. The birds at my feet were more interested in the crepes than in the fate of the statues and quickly devoured the crumbs as they fell to the ground.

Marie de Médicis might have sat in this exact spot almost four hundred years earlier, embracing the perfection of her creation. In that timeless location, I reread a letter I had been carrying in my pocket.

A month earlier, while working as a computer programmer, I had been responsible for entertaining Thierry
Lepage, the director of data processing from Milton Roy
Dosapro, a branch of our company that was located in
Normandy. For a week, we discussed the latest trends in
computers and compared the work being done in the two
branches. Before his departure, Thierry had left a letter on
my desk.

"Dear Barry, Thank you for spending the week with me
and helping me understand the programs you are working
on. I was very impressed. If you ever move to France and
learn the language, look me up. You'll have a job. Sincerely,
Thierry Lepage."

"If you ever move to France..." I thought I could never
move to another country on my own. I would have problems
with language, customs, finding an apartment, and who
knew what else? I wouldn't even know where to start.

The warm breeze stirred the leaves of the elm trees as
I sat below them, dreaming of a life in Paris.

The Invite

"The world is a great book, and those who do not travel read only one page."—St. Augustine

———— ♦ ————

THANKSGIVING IN PARIS - 1978

In the summer of 1978, a letter arrived from Switzerland. Heidi had offered to meet me for the Thanksgiving weekend at the Hôtel du Brésil, just outside the entrance to Luxembourg Gardens, near the Sorbonne campus of the University of Paris. She had some news she wanted to share. It would be nice to see Heidi again, but what was this news she had to share? And why didn't she just write it in her letter?

Barry Frangipane, Tampa to Miami to Paris, 1978

Upon returning to my hometown near Clearwater, Florida, I saw the same friends playing Frisbee on the beach, just as I had seen them before my departure to France. They had been playing volleyball in May, before my first visit to Paris. I was beginning to feel disconnected from them somehow, as if I was on a different path. As the sun set, we sat on the beach together and caught up.

"So, what have you been doing, Barry? Where have you been?"

"I just got back from another trip to Paris. And I'm planning to go back for Thanksgiving. Does anyone want to join me?"

"Paris? In France? Oh, I would give anything to be able to go to France."

Further conversations disclosed that my friends had each spent more money on movies, beer, eating out, and new car payments than I had spent on my two trips combined. I explained that my new unit of currency was "trips to Paris." A new car? Let me see. That would be four trips to Paris a year I would have to give up. No, thanks. My six-year-old Chevy Vega used more oil than gas, but as long as it ran, I would be saving four trips to Paris a year. I kept my car and planned for Thanksgiving. None of my beach friends would join me.

It was a busy Thanksgiving weekend, and the floor of Miami's airport was hard. The backpack cushioned my head as I napped briefly while waiting for my number to be called for a standby seat on the next flight to Paris. I had number four, and judging by the small number of passengers waiting at the gate, I was fairly certain I would make it aboard. I had flown from Tampa to Miami the night before and saved money by sleeping on the floor at the airport. The discomfort of the accommodations was no match for my dreams of being reunited with the City of Light. Paris was waiting, and I was ready to return to her.

"Number four!" The gate agent called my number, and I boarded the flight.

Once we landed at Charles de Gaulle airport, I metroed my way to the fifth arrondissement to the Hôtel du Brésil. Heidi was waiting for me in the lobby, excited about whatever she had to tell me. Our room was on the top floor and came complete with two single beds and no room for anything else. The ceiling slanted downward toward the window, so if you sat up too quickly—or in the wrong direction—you would smack your head on the ceiling. But it was Paris, and I was there.

THE INVITE

November in Paris is usually chilly, and this day was no exception. The café au lait helped keep me warm as Heidi and I sat outside Les Deux Magots, watching the world go by just as Ernest Hemingway frequently did in the café more than fifty years earlier.

"I have an idea." Heidi stared out at the sparse traffic on Boulevard Saint-Germain. She wasn't one for surprises, so I listened intently while keeping my hands wrapped around my coffee.

"I've got to return to Paris in January for my last year of studies at the Sorbonne and was wondering if you would like to stay here with me. You would have to learn French and help with expenses. Of course, I will be studying quite a bit, but it would be nice to have a roommate."

She finally turned toward me. "What do you think?"

"Did I just hear you ask me to join you for a year in Paris? Yes! Yes, of course! But, but... when, exactly?" I stammered like a fool.

Heidi laughed. "Let's go for a walk and talk about it."

Just a few meters away from the café stood an ornate

green cast-iron fountain almost ten feet tall with a cupola held up by four small statues of goddesses. Water flowed continuously, and tourists filled their water bottles.

"These fountains," Heidi said, "were donated by an Englishman named Sir Richard Wallace over one hundred years ago. There was a shortage of potable water for the working class, and many people drank alcohol rather than risk drinking from the Seine. Wallace designed and donated more than fifty fountains so that everyone could have clean water to drink. Silver cups hung from those hooks for years to give people an easy way to get a drink. The four women holding up the top of the fountain represent sobriety, kindness, charity, and simplicity."

"How do you know so much about this Wallace character?" I asked.

"In my three previous years at the University of Paris, I studied the history of the city. But enough about me. Let's keep walking, and I'll tell you the plan."

It was a short distance from Rue Bonaparte past the old homes of writers Henry Miller and Jean-Paul Sartre to the banks of the Seine. Even at that time of year, the bateaux mouches carried hundreds of tourists down the river, giving them a brief glimpse of the city where I had just been invited to live for a year.

Heidi explained, "I've got a few connections for possible apartments in the 13th Arrondissement. The 13th is a mostly residential neighborhood but close to the center. I'll be gone for a few weeks in the summer for mandatory boot camp in the Swiss Army but otherwise will be here for the year. School starts right after New Year's Day."

When we walked past Pont Saint-Michel, Notre Dame came into full view.

"But Heidi, that's six weeks from now. I won't even have time to get a visa."

She stopped walking. "You can stay for three months without a visa. Just be sure to visit another country every three months to have your passport stamped, showing you haven't spent the entire time in France."

As we walked along the Seine river, Heidi stopped in front of one of the green wooden boxes full of books sold by sidewalk vendors.

"These booksellers are called *bouquinistes*, and they've been selling used and rare books on both sides of the Seine since roughly 1600. With over three hundred thousand books, they stretch for over four kilometers along the riverbanks. French writer Jean Dutourd said that the Seine is the only river that runs between two bookshelves."

She paid for a small paperback and handed it to me. The cover had a drawing of a young boy carrying his books on the way to school. "This is for you," Heidi said. "It's called *Le Petit Nicolas* and is a humorous book about Nicolas and his views of the world. Sempé and Goscinny imparted their unique sense of humor to the characters. Make it your goal to understand the French inside. Since it's told through the eyes of a nine-year-old, the words should be easier for you to learn. When you have mastered this book, you'll have a working knowledge of the language. After all, if you're going to stay in France, you will need to truly understand

French."

I tucked *Le Petit Nicolas* inside my jacket pocket. As we continued our walk, the wheels started to turn.

There was my job at Milton Roy Corporation, which I would have to quit. What would I bring with me for a year? And my parents. God, I would have to tell them I was leaving the country. But there she was, Notre Dame, staring down at me, somehow assuring me that just as she had survived for over six hundred years, I, too, could survive in Paris for one.

"I'll have to get winter clothes," I told Heidi. "What I'm wearing now is my entire winter wardrobe."

That night at the hotel, I couldn't sleep. Staring out the window, I said, "Tomorrow, let's celebrate and go out to eat." Then I remembered that the next day was Thanksgiving and everything would probably be closed.

Heidi laughed. "Don't be silly. This is France. They don't celebrate Thanksgiving. There are no pilgrims and no Indians. But I do know a little restaurant where we can get turkey."

TELLING MY PARENTS

My excitement kept me awake throughout the entire flight home. Even in the last week of November, the humidity was stifling as I left the airplane and greeted my parents at the airport in Tampa. They were so used to me darting off to one place or another that picking me up after having been gone for a few days was nothing exceptional.

"Was midnight the only flight you could get to come home?" Dad asked.

"No, but it was the cheapest."

After unpacking in my bedroom, I placed a postcard of the Eiffel Tower on my nightstand and turned off the light. I would tell them in the morning.

The air in the kitchen was thick with the aroma of French roast coffee I had just finished brewing when my mother came in, wiping the sleep out of her eyes.

"It's only six o'clock in the morning. What are you doing up so early, especially after such a long flight?"

"Mom, let me tell you all about my trip." I filled her in on the details of the move, noting that it would only be for a year—although I really wasn't so certain—and that I would leave for Paris in six weeks. The money I'd saved would probably last me six months, then I could get a job. My mother was always happy for me whenever I ventured out into the world to expand my horizons. I was just twenty-one, and she felt this was a great opportunity. But she knew my father wouldn't be happy.

"Whatever you do, do not tell your dad. He almost had a heart attack when you announced that you were moving to Colorado for college. Imagine how he'll feel about his son moving four thousand miles away to another country!"

But as always, she had a plan to get Dad to agree.

"I'll make him his favorite dinner tonight, eggplant parmesan. We'll have some wine. I'll wear his favorite blouse. And then I'll break the news to him. You should probably leave the house for a while this evening."

My father, who smoked maybe one pack of cigarettes a year, was outside smoking and pacing when I returned home late after seeing the movie *Grease* that night.

"But why France? Why not Miami or Atlanta? What if you get sick way over there?"

My father and I were very close, and I knew he was more worried about how he would cope than he was about me. "Dad, if I get sick, I'll go to the doctor. The French invented X-rays, pasteurization, aspirin, and antibiotics. I'll be okay. And you'll be okay too. You'll have time together with Mom. Besides, I'm in love."

"You and Heidi?"

I groaned. "No, Dad. With Paris."

"I'll miss you, son. But I understand. It's a big world out there, and I can't expect you to spend your life here in Seminole, Florida. You will call, won't you?"

"Yes, Dad. I'll call."

My father's question made me laugh. "In love with Heidi?"

LE DEPART - JANUARY 1979

With a month having passed since my return to Florida, the departure date loomed. I took one last trip to the beach to tell my friends I was moving. Dressed in flannel shirts, jeans, and bare feet, they stopped their beach volleyball game just long enough to hear what I was saying.

"You're moving where?"

"Paris. You know, in France."

"You can't just move to France on a moment's notice," one of them said.

"Why not? Is there a law?"

"No, it's just that you've got to plan these things years in advance."

Very few of my friends had traveled outside of Florida, so the idea of going to France was strange to them.

"Well, I don't have years. I've got two weeks, just enough time to pack. Au revoir!"

I had already given my notice the week before at Milton Roy.

"We knew we couldn't keep you much longer," my boss had said. "You've had that wanderlust for quite a while now."

I laughed, thinking back. "That wanderlust," like it was some sort of disease.

There truly wasn't much time, so with the largest suitcase I could find perched on my bed, I started packing. But what does one pack for a year? I included only the most crucial items like some jeans, peanut butter, maple extract, and a ton of spices. My mother inspected the suitcase to be sure I had all the right things.

"Pure maple extract? What's that for? And peanut butter?"

"Mom, they don't have pancake syrup. I can mix the maple extract with corn syrup to make pancake syrup. And I've never seen peanut butter in France, so if I run low on money…"

She chuckled. "If you run out of money, you'll eat peanut butter and jelly? How do you know they have jelly?"

"Mom, they have jelly with their croissants. In fact, they have a saying, 'La vie est dure, sans confiture.'"

"And what on earth does that mean?"

"It means life is smelly without jelly," I said, paraphrasing.

Later, my parents and I chatted over a dinner of veal saltimbocca with polenta. I would miss them every day, I explained, but this was the opportunity of a lifetime. After dinner, I placed the last few items in my suitcase before my departure the next morning. The letter from Thierry Lepage sat next to my plane ticket on the nightstand. "If you ever move to France and learn the language, look me up. You'll have a job."

I read the letter one last time and placed it in the suitcase. Tomorrow would be the start of a long journey. While I was happy my travel agent had found such an inexpensive route to Paris, at that moment, Tampa to Miami to the Bahamas via Air Bahama then Icelandic Air to Luxembourg followed by a train to Paris was looking like quite the excursion. But it didn't matter. I was moving to Paris!

Living Together

After many flights, trains, and little sleep, I arrived in Paris.

———————— ✦ ————————

L'ARRIVÉE - JANUARY 1979

"Ouvrez la valise."

The policeman at the Gare de l'Est train station asked me to open my suitcase. It had sounded like such a good idea to check my bag in Luxembourg so that I could rest during the trip without worrying about my luggage. But now, retrieving my bag, I faced my worst fear—a policeman with a dog. I opened the suitcase slowly, but still, eight containers spilled onto the ground, each one holding tiny pieces of leaves. The policeman reached down and swooped up one. He opened it and placed it in front of his dog, who was not at all interested. After recapping the container marked

Thyme, he tried to interest his canine in the ones marked Oregano, Rosemary, Basil, and any of the other spices I had brought with me. Satisfied, he allowed me to close my suitcase and check it into storage. With the bag checked, it was a short Metro ride to the Saint-Michel station then to Notre Dame to meet Heidi.

As I was photobombing tourists in front of the cathedral, the bells rang twelve times. I had arrived an hour early, and at the agreed-upon time of noon, Heidi showed up to greet me. "Bonjour, mon ami! Are you ready to see our Parisian apartment?"

We ran down the steps to the Metro, changed at Denfert-Rochereau, and exited at Glacière. Walking Rue de la Glacière, we passed quite a few Chinese, Korean, and Vietnamese stores and restaurants. Menus in the windows offered pho, kimchee, dumplings, and many dishes I didn't recognize.

"The 13th is known as the Chinese neighborhood," Heidi explained. A short walk down rue Léon-Maurice-Nordmann took us to 6 Square Albin Cachot, which would be our home for the next year. The square was about half the size of a soccer field and surrounded by apartment buildings with six floors. Children kicked a soccer ball off one of the fountains.

"These apartments are fairly new, built in the 1930s. See that one on the far right? That's ours, number six."

I ran up the spiral staircase.

"Keep going. We live on the fourth floor. That's the fifth floor American!" Heidi hollered from behind me.

Square Albin Cachot, 1979

While I caught my breath outside our front door, she eventually arrived to unlock it, and we entered our three-hundred-square-foot apartment in Paris. It was spacious by Parisian standards—one 10' x 12' bedroom with two single beds and one 10' x 10' living-dining room. Both rooms had solid green carpeting and large French windows over-looking the courtyard. They were sparsely furnished with dark-wood decor that appeared to be from when the apartment complex was built. The apartment also had two skinny rooms no more than four feet across and twelve feet long. The first had a toilet and sink. The other had a small counter on one side and shelving on the other. Near the window were a sink, a tiny refrigerator with a hot plate on top, and a small rotisserie oven fastened to the wall above the hot plate. On the wall above the window was a shower nozzle.

"What's this?" I asked.

"Oh, that's the shower. Just unhook the basin from the wall, pull it down to the floor, and step in. Then pull the shower curtain around you, and... instant shower!"

Discovering that our shower was in the kitchen was the first of many surprises.

"Did you know that I could take a shower and flip pancakes on the hot plate at the same time?"

"I suppose you could," she said. "But watch out for the spattering grease! And besides, they don't have pancake syrup in France."

We were situated in a quiet part of the city, on the left bank. With our windows opening to the courtyard, we had very little street noise other than the laughter of children during the day and the occasional clatter of a woman's high heels as she walked home at night.

As the sun set over the square, I returned to Gare de l'Est to get my suitcase. It was a cold walk from Metro Glacière back to the apartment. Just outside Square Albin Cachot, there was a small 8 à Huit (open 8 a.m. to 8 p.m.) grocery store and a patisserie-boulangerie where we could get fresh bread and croissants each morning. Our apartment was in a perfect part of Paris. Exhausted, that night, I dreamt of the upcoming year, taking in all Paris had to offer, starting with two of those flaky croissants from the boulangerie downstairs.

PARIS PLAYS HARD TO GET

As the morning light filled our apartment windows, I awoke to the faint wails of police sirens in the distance. Heidi cracked open the window, providing further evidence of a city waking up. A look out over the courtyard showed garbagemen making their rounds and parents walking their children to school.

"Would you like me to get us some croissants for breakfast?" Heidi asked.

I appreciated her offer, but I was energized. Paris was my city now, and this would be a good opportunity for me to practice my limited French.

"Two croissants, please." This would be easy. As I walked down the stairs, I repeated out loud, "Deux croissants, s'il vous plait."

I left the building and skipped across the courtyard, repeating quietly, "Deux croissants, s'il vous plait."

Outside the boulangerie, I practiced one more time, "Deux croissants, s'il vous plait," and entered the store.

There were croissants of every type—large, small, chocolate-filled, whole wheat, almond, and more types of bread than I had ever imagined. The customer in front of me had purchased a baguette, delivered with no bag. Only a napkin graced the middle of the baton. The aromas of yeast, butter, and chocolate filled the air like thick perfume.

"Bonjour, madame. Deux croissants, s'il vous plait."

(There, I did it. Now I can just hand her this FF 10 note, get my change, and leave.)

Without handing me my croissants, the store owner replied.

"Est-ce que vous préférez les croissants grands, ou peut-être les petits? Nous avons aussi les croissants entiers. Lequel préférez-vous?"

I froze. I didn't understand a single word.

In the style of the famous French mime Marcel Marceau, I stopped talking and pointed at the croissants I wanted. The shopkeeper, who could tell I wasn't a local, chuckled, and I paid for my croissants and left.

"Au revoir, monsieur," she said as I ran out the door and back to the safety of my apartment. Conversing in French was going to be a little more difficult than I had expected.

Heidi had espresso waiting for me when I returned. She pulled her croissant apart slowly, and as the steam escaped, she advised, "Neither the French language nor Paris will come to you all at once. Just like this croissant, you must enjoy her slowly, one layer at a time."

While her words were welcomed, I was still embarrassed and decided that a nice warm shower might give me a better start to the day. As instructed, I unhooked the metal basin from the kitchen wall and pulled the shower curtain around it.

"Heidi," I called, "there's no hot water."

"Did you turn the water heater on? There's a small water heater on the wall. Hold down the button until the little light comes on, and the water will be warm in about fifteen minutes. After thirty minutes, the water heater shuts off automatically. Here in Europe, electricity is expensive, and we can't afford to waste it."

Within five minutes, I ran out of hot water. But after I enjoyed a bubbly hot chocolate, my body temperature returned to normal.

Later, I walked the neighborhood with Heidi, and we came upon what looked like a centuries-old fortress surrounded by armed guards. The fortress was only a block away from home, on Rue de la Santé.

"Heidi, these guards look serious. What is this place?"

"Oh, this is the Prison de la Santé. It's a maximum-security prison. We're pretty lucky to have this police presence in our neighborhood, don't you think?"

Feeling more curious than lucky, I asked, "How old is this prison?"

"It's over one hundred years old, built in the 1860s."

"Do they chop people's heads off in there with the guillotine?"

Prison de la Santé

Living Together

Heidi chuckled. "In the old days, yes, right in front of the prison. But no one has been guillotined here since 1972."

"But that was only seven years ago. You mean that in the late sixties, while we were burning bras in the streets in the USA, they were guillotining people here?"

At the guard station, Heidi asked the guard whether people had actually had their heads chopped off right where we were standing as recently as 1972.

Pointing at a spot about thirty feet away, the guard laughed. "No, madame. The guillotine was way over there."

Changing the subject, Heidi pointed down the street at Boulevard Arago.

"Speaking of burning bras, down that street is the old home of Simone de Beauvoir. In addition to founding existentialism with Jean-Paul Sartre, she was a significant voice in the women's movement both here in France and around the world. She wrote *The Second Sex* back in 1949, and that book started people thinking about equality for women. I think she still lives somewhere in this neighborhood."

Along Boulevard Arago, we passed a dark-green metal structure resembling a double phone booth but with no phones and no doors.

"This is an example of the inequality Simone de Beauvoir fought against. It's called a *pissoir* and is essentially a urinal for men. Since the 1830s, when Haussmann redesigned Paris, there were more than a thousand of these odorous stations for men to relieve themselves on their way to and from work, while women still had to wait until they got home to use a proper restroom."

"But there's no privacy. You can see right into it," I commented.

"I know. It's been said that these are the only restrooms where a man can pee with one hand while still holding hands with his girl with the other. Besides, they smell awful, and urine frequently runs onto either the sidewalk or the streets. On a positive note, during World War II, they were used as a place for the Resistance to share information on the locations of the Nazis. Fortunately, there is talk of finally replacing them with some sort of closed restrooms for use by both sexes."

We walked on to Le Select on Boulevard du Montparnasse, had a few cafés au lait, and discussed the coming months. It was obvious to Heidi after watching me order that my three years of high school French were getting me nowhere.

"There's a French school on Boulevard Raspail called Alliance Française. They've been teaching foreigners just like you for almost a century. You can go there every morning for a while until you really know the language."

The next day, I walked through Luxembourg Gardens toward Boulevard Raspail while eating my pain au chocolat. Quite a few people stood on the sidewalk. Movie cameras and microphones were at the ready. There were not, oddly, any actors, so I proceeded along my path to the school. A director type said something to me as I stepped into the street, but I couldn't understand him. This was partially due to my inability to understand French but also due to a loud noise coming from down the street. Just then, someone grabbed my shirt collar and dragged me back onto the curb as two cars came racing through the intersection with the cameras filming as my pastry flew out of my hand and was crushed by one of the vehicles. The director didn't seem at all pleased with the filming. As his crew reset the scene for another take, I looked sadly at my pastry being swept to the side of the road by the crew. With the intersection now safe from racing cars, my journey continued. Maybe taking real French lessons wasn't such a bad idea. It could be useful to understand phrases such as "We're filming a movie with cars traveling at a high velocity through the street. If you cross now, you might be killed."

An imposing six-story building with French flags flying and the words Alliance Française engraved in the stone façade greeted me upon my arrival at 101 Boulevard Raspail. Cars and buses rushed by, unaware that my future in Paris depended upon this building and how well I did inside of it.

After pausing to gaze at the structure that would become my home every morning for months, I went through the iron gate and to the reception desk just inside the door. Fumbling in French, I gave the receptionist my name and told her I wanted to improve my knowledge of the language. In perfect English, she directed me to go up the stairs, where a professor would give me a test to determine my starting class level. Handing me a stack of forms, she pointed at the grand staircase directly behind me and assured me that I would do fine.

I turned toward the staircase and froze. A group of students walked around me, chatting on their way to class. The receptionist called out, "Go on. It's okay."

Upstairs, I arrived at the testing desk. The smell of fresh-baked pastries filled the corridor, likely emanating from the student café visible down the hall. A professor reviewed my paperwork and explained in English, "Take this test and find a seat in the room across the hall. Do your best and return it to me after you've answered as many questions as possible."

About ten of us potential students were taking the test, our futures dependent upon the outcome. I sat in one of the metal frame desks with a wooden desktop resembling the ones in my fifth-grade classroom. Starting the test, I noticed that even the questions were in French, making it nearly impossible for me to complete. The professor scored my half-empty paper and put me in level two. I celebrated my inscription with a warm pain au raisin from the student café. The class would start the following Monday at 9 a.m. sharp and end at 1 p.m., leaving my afternoons free for me to enjoy Paris. The cost of the school was more than I expected, but I had my savings, so it would likely all work out. And besides, I needed to learn the language before I could get a job. Rushing back to the apartment to tell Heidi, I remembered her request for me to stop by the butcher at the corner of Rue L.M. Nordmann and Glacière.

"We need five hundred grams of veal cutlets, sliced thin," she had instructed.

Telling the butcher would be simple, I thought, since I already knew that the word for veal in French was "veau."

"Bonsoir, monsieur," greeted the butcher.

I froze. With no idea how to say "cutlets, sliced thin," I had no way to fill my order. Then I saw thinly sliced chicken cutlets in the display case. Pointing at the chicken, I blurted out, "cinq cent grammes, s'il vous plait."

I paid for my purchase and returned to the apartment a bit humiliated but armed with dinner.

"Barry, this isn't veal. It's chicken."

"Yes, I know. I'll order veal after I start school next Monday. Besides, chicken is healthier."

It was not the way I had intended to tell her about the start of my French lessons.

FRENCH CLASS

I was twenty-one but felt like a kid when Monday came around, apprehensive about the teacher and the school and wondering if I could make friends with students from other countries who spoke neither English nor French. A grand staircase led me from the world of a tourist into the beginning of my new life, learning French. In the class-room, I took a deep breath and found a seat.

A small lady in her late fifties with wiry red hair and a thin frame came in the door and walked straight to the chalkboard.

"Bonjour, mes étudiants. Je m'appelle Madame Ankaoua."

She wrote "Madame Ankaoua" on the board. Holding up the textbook to page seven, she said, "Ouvrez vos livres à la page sept."

At that point, it was evident that this French class was not being taught in English but in French. How could I learn French if I couldn't even understand her instructions? After four hours, I left in tears and decided to walk home through Luxembourg Gardens to lift my spirits. The gardens always cheered me up.

Inside the park, near the entrance on Rue Guynemer, four old men played bocce or *pétanque* as it was called here. They stared intently at the position of each ball before launching the one they spun in their hands. As their ball crashed into the others, their competitors remained expressionless, calculating how to toss their next ball. Their serious play was in complete contrast to the carefree children on the carousel just a short distance away. Although it was still January, the gardens were full of life as Parisians enjoyed the cold but sunny day.

After leaving Luxembourg Gardens, I stopped at the crepe stand to enjoy a butter-sugar crepe in the sun. Wiping the last bit of butter off my hand, I took the number 21 bus home. I could learn French. It would just take time.

A Student in Paris

SETTLING IN

Two weeks of French class had gone by, and I was settling into a routine. Each morning, I picked up a pain au chocolat at the boulangerie on Rue L.M. Nordmann, took the bus to Luxembourg station, and walked through Luxembourg Gardens. Then I would cut over to Boulevard Raspail toward Alliance Française. During breaks, I treated myself to a pain au raisin at the school cafeteria. The flakiness of the buttery dough combined with the aroma of the pastry cream and the sweetness of the raisins gave me fuel to stay in class. When school was over, I worked on my homework in the sun on one of those green metal chairs in the gardens. A crepe satiated me until I took the bus home.

The nearby grocery store, 8 à Huit, provided us with our daily groceries. A girl around seven years old often sat outside the store, and she always greeted me with "Bonjour, monsieur." Her parents, Marie-Thérèse and Daniel, ran the 8 à Huit. The mother, in her forties, was thin with straight pulled-back hair and glasses. The father was well-fed, with enough German in his looks to possibly be from the Alsace region of France. Marie-Thérèse rushed around the store and came out occasionally to warn, "Caroline, attention aux voitures," keeping young Caroline away from passing cars. Then she would bark, "Daniel, nous n'avons plus de lait," when the store was low on milk. Her speech was so fast that it was difficult for me to understand, although at that point, most Parisians spoke faster than I could comprehend. Caroline's older brother, Danny, helped out in the store but was very shy and mostly interested in staying out of the way of his parents.

Back at the apartment, I was warming up a can of stewed vegetables, known in France by the more elegant name of *ratatouille*, when the phone rang.

"Bonsoir."

"Allo, taxi?"

"Non, vous vous trompez, madame. Ce n'est pas un taxi."

"Je ne me suis pas trompée, monsieur. Je voudrais un taxi."

"J'en suis désolé, madame, mais je n'ai pas un taxi."

Heidi was returning from school just as I hung up the phone.

"Who was that?"

"Oh, just some lady wanting a taxi. When I told her she had dialed the wrong number, she became upset and demanded a taxi. I told her I didn't have a taxi and hung up while she was still insisting that she was right."

The next morning, school started with a jolt. "Put your hands up and don't move! This is a robbery!" Madame Ankaoua walked through the classroom while pretending her hand was a gun, ensuring all of us had our hands up. "Ne bougez pas!" she yelled if we moved.

I never imagined robbing a bank was something I would learn how to do in French class.

"Donnez-moi toute l'argent," Madame said, each of us pretending to empty our wallets for her.

She later explained that if there was a robbery and we didn't follow the instructions, we could be shot. Adel, a student from Iran, asked her to repeat the spelling of machine gun. M-i-t-r-a-i-l-l-e-t-t-e. Adel wrote it down quickly, having an exceptional interest in the day's lesson.

Although we were now educated in how to rob a bank, the night's homework was to describe a French food we enjoyed and explain why. There were so many diverse foods in Paris, I wondered what I would write about.

With February coming to an end, I was finding it easier to read newspapers and books in French, but the spoken word was still challenging. In the evenings, when Heidi wasn't busy with her lessons, she helped me with the oral homework, focusing on my pronunciation. The friends I had made at school were from Mexico, Iran, Germany, Canada, Greece, and Peru. Most spoke no English, so the only language we had in common was French. Using simple French combined with sign language, we did our best to communicate. Since we all spoke slowly, that made it easier to understand each other. During an outing to the Medici Fountain, Petra from Germany said, "Fifty years ago, when Ernest Hemingway was a poor writer living in Paris, he strangled the pigeons right here by this fountain and smuggled them out of the park in a baby carriage for dinner."

My frequent meal of canned ratatouille sounded pretty darn good.

Our French professor was strict about us doing our homework, so that night, I wrote about why eating ratatouille was better than eating fresh pigeon.

MULTICULTURAL PARIS

Petra sat on the bottom step of the grand staircase of the school, textbook on her lap, crying. Sitting down next to her, I asked if she was okay.

"I just don't get it."

"Get what, Petra?"

"He just got up and left!"

"Who? When?"

"Adel. He had asked for my help with his homework, and we were working together on his assignment. I was in the middle of a sentence when he just stood up and walked away without saying a word as if I wasn't even here."

"Petra, Adel is from Iran. In his country, a man would never be taught by a woman. Either he couldn't take the idea emotionally, or one of his Iranian friends was walking by and Adel didn't want to be seen getting help from a woman. We may never know."

With my limited German and her limited English, Petra and I worked on our homework together until the final school bell of the day indicated it was time to leave.

My walk home took me past the theater in Luxembourg Gardens. The children stood outside in unbridled anticipation of the marionette show. Puppet shows have been a tradition here since 1933, and it looked like a fun thing to do—having a puppet, that is. At the Boul' Mich' entrance to the park, an elderly lady sold dolls, small sailboats, balls, and puppets. I purchased a Popeye hand puppet. On the bus ride home, I practiced getting him to speak and use exaggerated gestures. "Je veux les epinards!" he growled, searching out the window for spinach while holding one hand above his good eye.

Near home, Caroline sat outside the 8 à Huit, enjoying a Toblerone chocolate bar, her snack of choice. Popeye sat with her and chatted while sharing the candy. It became a ritual for the three of us to sit outside the store after school. I frequently supplied the Toblerone, and she corrected Popeye's French.

Over the coming weeks, Popeye traveled with me in my backpack, and we practiced our French together by speaking to each other in the park. With my help, Popeye even purchased a newspaper at the local kiosk. He was a great conversation starter.

I explained to the newspaper vendor that Popeye was helping me practice my French. This started a conversation about foreigners who moved to Paris and didn't try to learn French.

He told me, "I've heard people say that we Parisians hate foreigners, and that's not true. It's just that when we ride the bus, take the Metro, walk the streets, or go to a restaurant, we rarely hear French anymore, and that gets a bit tiring after a while." He wished Popeye and me good luck in learning the language.

With Heidi studying day and night, I found myself spending more time with my classmates. Our French improving, four of us decided to rent a car and head to Normandy for a day. We had heard about the ruins of a twelfth-century castle in Les Andelys and an abbey built in 942 in Jumièges. I was looking forward to a day with my new friends.

After parking the car at the base of Château Gaillard, Adel, Petra, Tara (from Holland), and I ran up the ninety-meter hill to the ruins of the castle. Though little more than the thirty-foot-high walls of the château's keep remained, it was still an impressive structure. A pentagonal inner keep with curved exterior walls would have been easy to defend. The view looking down at the fog rising from the Seine river was stunning. The king could have seen for miles in every direction. I walked to the edge of the ruins and imagined Richard the Lionheart, king of England, looking down in 1198 from his new castle at the town of Les Andelys below. How content he must have been—right up until he died less than a year later after receiving an arrow in his shoulder. Adel walked up next to me and stared out at the distant horizon. He was a quiet kid, about eighteen. I wondered what he was thinking as he looked down from this ancient castle.

"Adel, ça va?"

He thought for a moment then said, "The Iranian revolution will not be over until the Shah is dead."

We sat in silence for a few minutes. I asked no more questions, and Adel made no further political declarations.

It was lunchtime when we arrived in the town of Jumièges to see the Benedictine monastery built more than one thousand years before our arrival. At the local café, we ordered sandwiches. I was longing for a croque monsieur— a hot ham-and-cheese sandwich topped with béchamel sauce and broiled Gruyère cheese. But out of respect for Tara, who didn't eat meat, I selected a simple sandwich of a baguette with cheese, though I quickly discovered the cheese was a pungent Roquefort that had the power to keep vampires away. "Next time," I told myself, "I'm getting the croque monsieur."

The abbey at Jumièges had once housed more than a thousand monks. Since the French Revolution, however, it hadn't housed anyone, as it was missing the roof. Still, I was humbled by this structure, which over its ten centuries had incorporated Gothic, Roman, and Norman styles into its arches and columns. Victor Hugo, author of *The Hunchback of Notre Dame*, called it "the most beautiful ruin in France," and I had to agree. Even though little other than the exterior walls remained, in this quiet setting surrounded by trees, some of them over five hundred years old, I could easily imagine the monks hard at work back in the 600s. How different this was from where I grew up in Florida, where most everything had been built in the last thirty years.

The abbey was a massive structure, likely four stories tall when it was in operation. It was a lesson in our own mortality to see such a structure that had remained functional for most of the ten centuries before the French Revolution.

Tara called out, "C'est l'heure!"

Indeed, it was time to head back. We were three hours from Paris and had to return the rental car before the agency closed. The four of us piled into the Citroen. On the drive home, we—two Iranians, a German, and an American—sang, "Alouette, gentille Alouette" at the top of our lungs.

The orange sky and the setting sun painted a magical glow on the streets of Paris. As we returned our car and went our separate ways, I thought about how simple it seemed for people of different cultures to get along.

Once I was back at the apartment, the phone rang again. So many people insisted that they had indeed called the taxi service that I had started answering the phone, "Allo, taxi."

I reassured the caller, "Oui, oui, cinq minutes. Un chien? Oui, d'accord. Au revoir, madame."

"Who was that on the phone?" asked Heidi. "And what was that about a dog?"

"Oh, just someone wanting a taxi. I let her know that it wouldn't be any problem at all for her to bring her dog and that the taxi would arrive in about five minutes."

Heidi laughed. "I think you're starting to get the hang of living in Paris!"

LE MARCHÉ

During an early Saturday morning walk on Rue de la Glacière, I heard only the sounds from the feet of a lone jogger and water pouring from the garden hose of a shopkeeper cleaning off the sidewalk in front of her hardware store. Flowers started to awaken in pots adorning every window and opened with the fervor of a butterfly emerging in full color from its cocoon. The neighborhood street market was a feast for the senses with its colorful displays of fresh produce, fragrant flowers, and mouth-watering meats and cheeses from every corner of France and beyond. A vendor tried to interest me in his ripe grapefruit. The box said in English, "Grapefruit, Indian River, Florida."

"Monsieur, deux tomates, s'il vous plait," a frail woman in a white sweater and long black skirt told the young man selling fruit.

Over the past weeks, I had come to recognize most of the customers at the market. This elderly lady lived across the square from us and appeared to live alone. Another woman with well-kept short gray hair and a gray sweater was always accompanied by her husband, who used a walker and struggled to keep up. But last Wednesday and again that day, she was by herself, dressed in black. Young mothers brought their babies in strollers but appeared to be too rushed to enjoy the market.

Some of the street markets were more specialized, like the marché aux oiseaux on Île de la Cité, where finches, canaries, roosters, and chickens had been sold for hundreds of years. There was the marché aux puces, or flea market, with a variety of used goods, and the marché aux fleurs for the best selection of flowers and exotic plants. I had no need for birds, exotic plants, or fleas, so my local neighborhood market sufficed.

Using the French I learned at school, I made my way around the market. It was exciting to be able to ask questions and understand the responses when making purchases. I went home with blood oranges, butter from Normandy, an ash-encrusted goat cheese, and a dozen tulips. Each week, I chose the most vibrantly colored flowers to brighten our apartment, placing them by the bedroom window overlooking the courtyard below.

"Heidi, I have a question," I said. "Sometimes at the markets, a few of the vendors post crazy prices. This cheese had a price of twelve hundred francs. That's about two hundred dollars for a hunk of cheese. But when I asked the old man the price, he said twelve francs. So why do they post a price a hundred times the real price?"

Heidi laughed. "Those are the prices in old francs. In 1960, the French franc was redenominated. That means that new francs were issued with a value exactly one hundred times that of the old francs. And even though that was almost twenty years ago, some of the elderly vendors still quote prices in francs anciens or old francs. By the way, are those blood oranges you bought?"

"Yes, from Italy. Why?"

Heidi held up the day's newspaper containing a story about an Italian who was recently murdered by someone who had poisoned the blood oranges at his local market. Our oranges sat in a basket in the living room for about a week before we threw them away, neither one of us willing to risk being poisoned.

SPEECHLESS

While Heidi attended her evening class at the Sorbonne, I prepared a ham-and-melted-Gruyère sandwich on a demi-baguette in our tiny kitchen. As usual, I tried to improve my comprehension of the language by listening to the radio.

"FIP Radio, the time is seven o'clock. Tonight, at the Palais de Chaillot, Marcel Marceau will show three silent films from his private collection and speak to his students about the art of mime. The lecture begins at seven thirty and is open to the public."

Marcel Marceau, the father of modern mime, was speaking that night in Paris? I shut off the oven, left Heidi a note, and ran to the Glacière Metro station. After exiting the Metro line at Trocadero, I found three elderly ladies waiting outside the door of Le Palais. Before long, a slender man with wiry gray hair opened the door and motioned us inside. His toned body contrasted with his weathered face. The man ran up the stairs to the mezzanine and, looking down at us, greeted the newcomers. I found a seat among the dozen or so students in the small oval auditorium.

The man in the mezzanine spoke. "Bonsoir, mesdames et messieurs. My name is Marcel Marceau. Thank you for joining my students and me for tonight's lesson on the history of modern mime. I will be showing some films this evening from my home collection, starting with *La Vague* and ending with *Scrooge* by Charles Dickens."

For the next four hours, we watched as the master of mime explained his personal journey through the craft, each movie followed by questions from the audience. One of the students, apparently from Italy, asked his question in Italian, and Marceau responded in kind. I asked my questions in French, but he responded in English. (Evidently, my French had a way to go before becoming fully conversational.) Marceau's last film, *A Christmas Carol*, was a silent masterpiece in which he played all seventeen roles.

Taking the Metro home, I reflected on what I had experienced that night. Paris had a lot to teach me, and I was listening intently.

POP ROCKS

The 1890s posters of the Parisian cabarets drawn by Toulouse-Lautrec and Jules Chéret were stunning. Voluptuous women beckoning us to the Moulin Rouge, Folies-

Bergère, and Le Chat Noir depicted a time of gaiety in the city. I was in a new museum of posters, Le Musée de l'Affiche on Rue de Paradis, which had just opened a year earlier. In those days, posters rather than TV commercials enticed people to travel by train to exotic locations such as Chamonix in the winter and Nice in the summer.

While daydreaming of all the places beckoning me to their romantic doorsteps, I remembered a lunch appointment with Demetri, one of my Greek friends from school, who had invited me to his apartment near Place de la République. The city was eerily quiet as I approached Boulevard Saint-Martin. The entire boulevard was devoid of cars and pedestrians on that Saturday morning, except for me walking down the center of the street. In what was typically one of the busiest parts of Paris, it was quiet enough for me to hear the Pop Rocks candy exploding in my mouth as I walked.

In the distance ahead, I saw protesters in front of, around, and on top of the statue at Place de la République. They held banners and chanted unintelligible words from five hundred meters away. As I neared, the crowd appeared to grow larger and the chanting louder. I detoured into a side street, but a policeman blocked the way. Thinking that the situation could quickly get out of control, I turned back in the direction of Place de l'Opéra. After I went a short distance, three large blue buses arrived and blocked the road ahead. Immediately, dozens of riot police descended from the buses and prepared their gear. I tossed the rest of the candy in my mouth while trying to decide which direction to take. There was nowhere to go. Then I heard the gunshots.

"Venez! Venez vite!" The shopkeeper at the hair salon along Boulevard Saint-Martin had unlocked his door and was calling me inside. He locked the door behind us and motioned me to the back of the store. For the rest of the afternoon, I hid from view along with the shopkeeper, two women in curlers, and their hairdressers. We heard more gunshots, people chanting and screaming, and glass breaking, and we saw plenty of smoke and confusion when we dared to peek out the front window.

Darkness had descended and the crowds had vanished when we finally ventured outside. I walked down streets full of broken protest signs, garbage, and occasionally shattered glass from storefront windows. The smoke was clearing but burned my eyes nonetheless. After arriving at Demetri's apartment just in time for dinner, I shared my stories of the day while he prepared lamb chops with olive oil and oregano. Evidently, the steelworkers union had organized the "manifestation," and tens of thousands of protesters had been bused in from all parts of the country. Tear gas had been used to disperse the crowd, and dozens of people had been injured.

The midnight bells chimed as I arrived home. Heidi was already in bed.

"Barry, did you hear about the big protest today on the right bank? I hear it was pretty dangerous over there."

Somehow, I hadn't felt afraid but energized by a population willing to speak out. At the same time, I was annoyed by the non-Parisians who had left our city in such a mess. Though school was out for the weekend, I still learned quite a bit about French politics that day. I hoped the rest of March would be calmer and less educational. Paris, however, had other plans.

TERRORISTS STRIKE PARIS

The flowers were in full bloom and exceptionally colorful on one sunny March afternoon. As I sat at the Fontaine de Medicis in Luxembourg Gardens, the words of Madame Ankaoua's discussion of the morning came back to me. Algeria, her birthplace, had become an unfriendly place for Jews like her in the 1960s, so she relocated to Paris with her husband. Paris, she had said, welcomed them and gave them a new life. "How terrible it must be to leave your homeland due to persecution," I thought. It did seem, however, that the couple had adjusted well to life in France. Just the day before, Madame Ankaoua had shared her recipe for the perfect French crepe. Paris was inviting not only to me but also to countless others who were no longer welcome in their birthplaces.

While international news was still difficult for me to understand, it would have been hard to miss the newspaper headlines about Israel and Egypt signing an historic peace treaty. The future might be better for people such as Madame Ankaoua.

The #21 bus arrived at Luxembourg station just as I finished my chocolate-banana crepe. There was still space on the sun-filled open platform at the back of the bus, so I got in. As I glanced back at the Medici fountain, a huge explosion hit Rue de Medicis. Glass flew onto the street, cars drove off the road, and people ran for cover. Our bus driver veered south on Rue Gay-Lussac, leaving the area as quickly as possible.

Video of the scene played repetitively on the evening news. The images graphically displayed the terror brought upon Paris earlier in the day. Heidi helped translate the details of the story, which I couldn't yet understand.

Ambulances lined up to carry away the wounded from the Jewish restaurant on Rue de Médicis, almost directly across the street from the fountain I had visited just moments before the blast. Roughly thirty people were injured, many of them Jewish students on their lunch breaks. The evening turned icy cold, but more than a thousand people stood in solidarity with the injured outside on Rue de Médicis and, like me, pondered the meaning of the day's events. Meanwhile, an Islamic terrorist group claimed responsibility for the bombing. My thoughts were with Madame Ankaoua, and I wondered what she must have been feeling as she watched this story of hatred unfolding on television.

Growing up in a small Florida town, I had never seen this kind of vitriol expressed so violently against individuals the bombers had likely never met. I closed my eyes and thought, *Paris, please stop. I don't want to learn anything else today.*

TREMIL, ICELAND

Tennis was on the mind of Madame Ankaoua on one April day, and she was anxious to get to the courts in Jardin du Luxembourg now that the temperature approached sixty degrees Fahrenheit. Indeed, the park was full of children directing their model sailboats on the lake. Tulips filled the many flower beds, and sporty locals played tennis on the courts bordering Rue Guynemer. That day, I thought, would be a good day for an extended walk in the Latin Quarter. Walking past the Sorbonne, I found students outside preparing some sort of protest signs that read, "Non au Nucleaire." After recalling the prior month's protests, I made a mental note to avoid the Sorbonne on my way home in case this protest was also greeted by riot police.

On Rue des Écoles, the movie theater Action Ecoles was showing the Marx Brothers film *A Night at the Opera* in V.O., which stood for "Version Originale," in this case English. Based on the signs under the marquee, this theater showed almost exclusively Marx Brothers films in rotation, in English.

I wondered if the slapstick humor of the Marx Brothers would be appreciated in France. As I found my seat, the chatter of the audience was almost entirely in

French. The topic of improperly translated movies had made the press in recent days. While the subtitles were in French, they rarely matched the English dialogue. In fact, one famous subtitle gaffe was of a war movie in which tanks were coming over the hill, causing the star to announce "Tanks!" while the subtitle read "Merci!" or thanks.

The long walk home took me down Rue Mouffetard, a long street that wound through the Latin Quarter. "Le Mouffe," as it was called by the locals, was full of cafés and restaurants serving food from every corner of the globe. Heidi had told me it was more than two thousand years old, one of the oldest streets in Paris. It was a microcosm of almost everything gastronomic that Paris had to offer, all in less than half a mile. At the top of the hill was Le Volcan, with boeuf bourguignon and duck confit, followed by the shawarma of a small Lebanese restaurant, and Casa Pepe's Spanish paella. Indian vindaloo could be found directly across the street from a British pub. Near Place de la Contrescarpe, I stopped to look up at what had been Hemingway's home in 1922. Nothing special distinguished this building from any of the surrounding apartment buildings except for a small plaque which read, "It was the Paris of our youth, the times when we were very poor and very happy." At that moment, I understood his emotions completely.

A few doors away was a restaurant with a fully cooked pig wearing sunglasses and staring out the window. This part of the quarter was a favorite spot for students, but they were absent on this Monday evening. After reviewing the money left in my wallet, I skipped the Vietnamese pho, grabbed a crepe, and went home.

The nightly news was full of images from Paris and around the world of those protesting nuclear power. A picture of a smoking nuclear cooling tower was shown throughout the broadcast. I still found it difficult to understand the news, as they spoke extremely fast, but one thing I understood clearly—something important had happened in Iceland in a town called Tremil. Even American President Jimmy Carter was shown being escorted in and out of some sort of nuclear control room in Tremil, Iceland. This was undoubtedly related to the students protesting earlier in the day near the Sorbonne.

The next morning, I went to the local café to grab a croissant and the newspaper. While the vocabulary used in the daily paper was considerably more advanced than that of the TV news, the paper was easier for me to comprehend, reading at my own pace. As I downed my café au lait, the headline popped out: "Incident Nucleaire à Three Mile Island." It turned out there was no town called Tremil in Iceland. It was simply the French pronunciation by the newscaster reporting on a nuclear plant disaster at the Three Mile Island facility near Harrisburg, Pennsylvania, in the United States. While concerned for the people of Pennsylvania, I was happy to see that the people in Iceland were safe and sound.

VOYAGE TO SOMEWHERE

It was a great time to be in Paris. Cloudless skies and comfortable temperatures had replaced the cold rainy days of winter. The city had an unexplained energy. Passersby were happier and more talkative as a group of us students enjoyed an afternoon drink outside Café Le Luxembourg on Boul'Mich'. Popeye and I carried on quite a conversation, to the delight of the other students.

Pauline, a student from Canada, took control of the Popeye puppet and said, "Popeye, I am the gendarme. Do you have a visa to be here in France?"

"No, gendarme, I do not."

"Off to jail, then!"

"We're students. We don't really need a visa, do we?" I asked Pauline.

"Yes. Even as a student, you can only stay for three months without a student visa, which must be obtained in your home country."

Every three months, my fellow students explained, they left France and obtained a passport stamp from another country. This proved they had not been in France for the entire period. "But," I asked, "how do you guarantee that if you leave France, another country will stamp your passport? I traveled to Switzerland and Italy a few years ago, and no one stamped my passport at the border crossing. And I certainly can't afford to return to the United States."

"You can't ever be sure," said Demetri. "But there is one way…"

"What is it? Tell me, Demetri!"

"No, it's a lot of trouble."

I started sweating. "Demetri, whatever it is, I'll do it. I don't have to go to Greece, do I?"

Demetri laughed then called us all in close. He whispered the plan as I took notes.

The next morning, as instructed, I took the first train to Brussels, Belgium. Quickly, I hopped on a local train to Bruges, walked to the bus station, and purchased a ticket to somewhere far north of Belgium. Demetri had written the name of the city on a scrap of paper, which I handed to the ticket agent.

A cool breeze made its way through my light jacket as I boarded the bus. Once seated, I checked my day pack to be sure I had my lunch. One baguette with Brie, two apples, and a drink box with chocolate milk. I was ready for the journey north and settled in for the ride. The French road signs quickly gave way to those in a language I couldn't identify. As the hours ticked by, frost appeared on the inside of my window, and the villagers we passed were dressed for winter. Then, just as Demetri had described, the bus made its final stop, and all remaining passengers, including myself, descended.

My jacket and thin blue jeans were no match for the icy mist coming from the ocean in front of me. A sign at the waterfront read, "Nord Søen—NordSee—Nord Sjøen." Possibly, this was the North Sea. No wonder it was cold! Inside the bus station, I attempted to purchase a cup of coffee, but they didn't accept French francs, Belgian francs, or US dollars. Nor did they speak French or English. So, I sat inside per Demetri's instructions for one hour until the southbound bus started to board. "This is it," I said to myself. "I sure hope his plan works."

The bus left the station, and I kept careful track of the time. After a few hours, as expected, the bus stopped at a small house at the edge of a flat two-lane road with no other structures for miles. An elderly lady boarded the bus as I got off. "What time is the next bus?" I asked the driver, just to confirm.

"Six o'clock, and that's the last bus until tomorrow morning, so don't miss it."

Nervous and with fingers crossed, I entered the house. A middle-aged man sporting a mustache and well-pressed uniform sat behind the desk, clearly engrossed in paperwork. He looked over his glasses at me and said something in some language other than French or English. I responded in French. "Hello, sir. I was wondering if you might stamp my passport." I took a deep breath and handed him the document.

As he reached for the passport, I expected to see him pull out his stamp and ink pad, put the ink to the paper, and make my journey a success. Instead, he laid it back down.

Switching to French, he asked, "Why, son, would you want a passport stamp from me?"

It was awfully warm in his office. Surely, he could see me sweat. "Well, sir," I improvised, "please look at my passport. I'm collecting passport stamps, and as you can see, I only have stamps from the United States, France, and Italy. I would love to have a stamp from your fine country." In reality, I had no idea what fine country I was in.

He flipped through the passport, smiled, and placed a stamp on the first empty page. I quickly tucked it back in my pocket and thanked him profusely.

He interrupted, "It's five o'clock. I'm going home." After walking me outside, without another word, he got in his rusty Citroen and left. As in, he left me outside this small building at the side of a road, on the border between two countries, with nothing else for miles. I stood in the cold air, eating my last apple, when it started to rain.

At 6:02 p.m., a bus appeared in the distance. Not wanting to miss my last chance to escape, I stood in the center of the road and waved frantically. The driver was still yelling at me as I found my seat, but I wasn't listening. I had my passport stamp and was out of the rain and on my way back. Sleep came easily that night in my Bruges hostel. The bed was warm, and my clothes dried on the radiator.

Early the next morning, I arrived by train in Brussels to take the TGV to Paris. An announcement came over the loudspeakers. "The express train back to Paris is leaving from track two in three minutes."

Finally, I headed home to Paris. The rhythm of the rails rocked me into a deep sleep as the farms became greener going south. Awakened abruptly, I saw two then three gendarmes run down the corridor toward the next car. Some of the passengers were running in the opposite direction of the gendarmes. Then I noticed we were surrounded by farmland, and the train was no longer moving. There were no stations in view. Curious, I headed toward the police.

"Sit down, now!" one officer shouted at me as I passed through the first-class cars.

"Qu'est-ce qui ce passe?" What's going on, I asked one of my fellow first-class passengers. He pointed at the window.

"Someone shot at the moving train, and the gendarmes are doing an investigation."

My new seatmate also lived in Paris. We hardly noticed the departure of the gendarmes nor the movement of the train as we enjoyed each other's company and the comforts of first class.

Once I was back in Paris that night, Heidi examined my passport as I skewered pieces of skirt steak and dipped them in the hot oil to cook.

"Look at the stamp, Heidi. Where was I?"

She studied it. "I don't know. The date is clear, but the other words are blurred out as if the page had gotten wet before the ink dried."

I still have that passport and the hard-earned stamp, and I still have no idea what fine country it came from.

Working in Paris

NO MORE ENGLISH

Our walks together were becoming more frequent as Heidi's schoolwork lightened. I started to feel something more than a strong friendship for her but didn't want to say anything. I'd never had a steady girlfriend, so this was awkward. Heidi was five years older than I was and probably wouldn't be interested in us being more than just roommates. It would take time for me to decide what to say or whether to even bring up the topic at all.

While on one of our walks along the banks of the Seine, I noticed a bouquiniste offering many books of the Le Petit Nicolas series, including *Le Petit Nicolas and His Friends*, *Le Petit Nicolas on Vacation*, and *Le Petit Nicolas at Recess*.

Heidi commented, "As your French improves, you can come back here and add to your collection. Reading these books will help you increase your vocabulary and have fun at the same time."

After I purchased a copy of *Le Petit Nicolas and His Friends* and placed it in my backpack, a building with a large clock across the street caught my eye. It was a train station I had never seen before, although there didn't seem to be any passengers—or trains for that matter.

"That's Gare d'Orsay. It was built for the Paris-Orleans train route around 1900, with fully electric tracks. Many people feel that it's the most beautiful station in Paris. It has a gilt clock towering over the main hall. I wish you could see it!"

"Could we go there now?" I asked.

"No. Unfortunately, the station is too small for today's trains and has been closed for a few years now. There's talk of turning it into a museum, but don't hold your breath. That would be quite an undertaking."

We continued our walk to the Latin Quarter.

Heidi continued. "Did you know that when Ernest Hemingway lived in Paris, he would frequently come to this bookstore, Shakespeare and Company, and borrow books from the owner?"

She pointed out the famous bookstore as we walked toward Notre Dame.

"Borrow books from the store?" I asked. "Why didn't he just go to the library?"

Heidi explained, "Shakespeare and Company was one of the few places where Hemingway could find books written in English."

"But if he was living in Paris, why didn't he just learn French?"

"That's what I wanted to talk to you about today. Allons-y. Let's go to Bertillon for ice cream."

Passing through the park behind Notre Dame on the way to Île Saint-Louis, we stopped for a moment to sit on a bench and admire a garden of roses in full bloom, almost entirely ignored by the throngs of tourists at the front of the cathedral.

"Barry"—Heidi looked me straight in the eye—"tu ne peux pas continuer parler à me en anglais."

"What do you mean, I can't continue to speak English? I speak English, and you speak English. Why do we need to speak French to each other?"

Nervous, I got up off the bench and walked slowly toward Île Saint-Louis and the comfort of a fraise des bois ice cream cone.

Heidi followed right behind me and explained, "I've been doing you a disservice. You'll never fully know French if we keep speaking English, and you'll never be able to fully appreciate France without a better understanding of the language."

Heidi was right. As we left Bertillon, the sweetness of the tiny wild strawberries in my cone belied the bittersweet idea of speaking nothing but French to each other, even in the privacy of our apartment.

"Okay, Heidi. I have an idea. How about we speak French in the morning and English in the evening? I'm too tired at night to translate."

"No. You see, the problem is that you're still *translating*. With a bit more practice, you'll be thinking in French, and translation won't be necessary. You'll see. And you won't be so tired either. Tu vois ce que je veux te dire?"

"Okay, I see what you're saying, and I'll give it a try."

"Good. Work on your French. I'm proud of what you've accomplished so far. Just keep at it. I've got to head back and study. A bientôt."

As Heidi walked away, I imagined that I had heard the last words she would ever say to me in English. A walk to my favorite train station might cheer me up, I thought.

Paul Edward Theroux once said, "I sought trains. I found passengers." Gare de l'Est was bustling as usual. The shops were full of people making last-minute purchases, and even the café was nearly bursting with people—each one carrying luggage full of old clothes and fresh dreams. Travelers trading paradises. An Indian couple headed to London for a new start. Two Brits had just arrived in Paris for their honeymoon. A French family was returning from a ski trip.

There's no better place to study humanity than in a train station. Passengers depart either full of sadness or full of excitement.

The train carriage windows framed faces looking out at the platform, each face with its own story. Were they joining their loved ones? Visiting a grandchild for the first time? Were they starting a once-in-a-lifetime vacation or heading off to war? Those they left behind on the platform waved as the train slowly pulled away, then their heads hung as the train left the station. A train arrived from Zurich. Business-men and women descended quickly and beelined it to the taxi stand. Families with small children scurried to the Metro. And one woman, possibly in her late twenties with long curly brown hair hiding her face, anxiously waited for someone special to exit the train. As the crowd thinned, she looked up and down the platform and peered into the train windows, car by car. Suddenly, she turned around at the sound of her name, and an older woman with short gray hair and a dark complexion awaited. They embraced. With the younger woman carrying the luggage, the two walked toward the exit.

Reenergized after a few hours of studying humanity, I left the station and took the Metro to Place Saint-Michel and Créperie des Arts for a Crêpe Normande and a bowl of cider.

Outside the restaurant stood a young tourist with a copy of Frommer's *Europe on $10 a Day* in his hands, obviously lost. He looked carefully at the numbers on the buildings then back at his guidebook. Thinking this would be a great time to try Heidi's new "no more English" policy, I asked him if he needed help, but in French.

"Puis-je vous assister?"

"I don't speak French!" he barked back at me.

"Okay," I said very slowly. "Shall we try English? Do you need help?"

"It's these darned French. You know they hate Ameri-cans. They're trying to charge me almost a hundred dollars for a hotel room. The French can go to hell for all I care!"

I explained that trying to get a room in Paris at 8 p.m. on a weekend wasn't a great idea to start with, as typically, the only rooms left are the larger, more expensive ones. Once again, I offered to help.

"Let's do this. We'll walk into a hotel together, you ask for a room, and I'll help as needed."

The hotel clerk greeted him as he entered the hotel.

"Bonsoir, monsieur."

"Got a room?" he asked abruptly and too quickly for her to understand.

"Pardon, monsieur?"

"GOT A ROOM?" That time, he yelled. It was obvious to him that the real problem was that the French were deaf! No wonder the prices were so high. Taking control of the situation, I glared at the tourist and pointed at a chair in the lobby. "Sit there and don't say another word."

In French, I apologized to the woman behind the desk. "He's a young student from America, and he doesn't understand why the entire world doesn't speak English." She laughed, thanked me for helping, and gave him a room for roughly thirty dollars.

Before the night was over, I had returned to the hotel with a couple from Newcastle who needed a room and were hungry as well. There was no restaurant in the hotel, but the clerk made them each a ham sandwich on a fresh baguette before giving them the keys to their room. After returning to our apartment just past midnight, I woke Heidi to explain everything that had happened, in French. She smiled, closed her eyes, and said, "Bonne nuit."

"Bonne nuit, Heidi," I replied.

It had been a good day. Maybe that night, I thought, would be a good time to tell her how I felt about her.

"Heidi," I would say, "I've fallen in love with you."

I sat, thinking about how to say it in French, then I heard her snoring.

Perhaps it would be better to wait for another day.

SPEND A WEEKEND WITH A FRENCH FAMILY

As the days grew longer and the temperatures warmer, my desire to see other areas of France grew. Alliance Française had a program entitled "Spend a Weekend with a French Family" that assigned a student to a family living a few hours outside of Paris. The family got an opportunity to meet someone from another culture, while the student expanded their knowledge of France and practiced speaking French at the same time. After discussing my options with a school counselor, I chose a family in Vannes, a coastal town in Brittany.

Late Friday afternoon, my train arrived in Vannes. As the passengers collected their bags, children, souvenirs, spouses, and remaining food items, they departed the station, leaving only me on the platform.

"Barry?"

I turned around to see a woman in her forties with a dark complexion and short auburn hair.

"So sorry I'm late," she said in French, explaining something about her teenage son and daughter helping her clean her house before my arrival.

"Hi, I'm Odile." She placed my backpack in the trunk of her Citroen before speeding toward her home in the port of Vannes.

A cool sea breeze greeted us while we walked from the parking lot through the port to get to the house. The smell of seafood filled the air, and its source was a man on the street who was stirring a five-foot-diameter pan that bubbled with hot paella. Locals lined up for their dinner, a combination of rice and whatever fresh seafood was caught that day.

Odile's sixteen-year-old son, Jean, and fourteen-year-old daughter, Anne, were excited to meet me. Jean was holding a Fleetwood Mac album and started to ask me something when Odile said, "Put the record down. It can wait. Set the table while Anne and I finish preparing dinner."

When the meal was ready, she said, "Tonight, we've made a typical Brittany dinner. Cauliflower in a salted butter-and-cheese sauce, crab-stuffed avocado, and fish cooked in a butter-wine sauce. This beurre blanc sauce was invented over a hundred years ago only an hour from here in Saint-Julien-de-Concelles. Jean, pour Barry a bowl of our local cider."

I navigated the cauliflower with no problem, but the avocado was new to me. At twenty years old, I had never eaten an avocado. It wasn't in my mother's repertoire. But it looked a lot like a crab-stuffed baked potato, so I wasn't really concerned until Jean poked Anne while pointing at me and laughing.

Odile could see the confused look on my face as she said, "In France, we don't eat the rind of the avocado. Isn't it a bit tough?"

Realizing my mistake, I chose to leave the rest of the avocado skin on my plate. It turned out to be a much more pleasant dish without it.

After we finished the strawberry-topped kouign-amann, a special Brittany butter cake, Jean returned with the Fleetwood Mac album. He played the song "Rhiannon" and handed me the album cover.

"Could you please translate this song for me? We can't figure out the lyrics."

Jean looked quite disappointed when I explained, "I've probably listened to that song a hundred times and still can't understand a word she's saying. It's possible that Stevie Nicks didn't know them either and just mumbled as she sang so no one would catch on."

He took the album off the record player and never brought it out again.

Over coffee, we discussed some of the differences between growing up in Florida and in Vannes. Anne was surprised that I had to pay for my college education, while Jean liked the fact that I could drive legally at fifteen. It was refreshing to be able to converse in French with these two teenagers without too much difficulty.

The sound of the gulls in the harbor conspired with the cool ocean breeze to lull me into a deep sleep. In the morning, the dull rumbling of boats heading out to sea was drowned out by Odile telling everyone to wake up and prepare for a trip to a nearby island.

"Belle-Île is roughly ten kilometers off the coast," she explained. "We'll take the ferry and have lunch in the port of Le Palais."

On board the ferry, Odile noticed me gazing at an island the boat was passing with quite a few tourists milling about its harbor.

"That's Île-aux-Moines. Tourists like it because it's small enough that you can see the whole island by bicycle in an hour or two. But we're not going there. Our destination is still some kilometers away."

As we left the Gulf of Morbihan and headed onto open waters, the wind whipped the ocean against the lighthouses along the way to Belle-Île-en-Mer. After the ferry docked, Odile rented a car while Jean, Anne, and I enjoyed galettes in the port.

"A galette is nothing more than a fancy name for a buckwheat crepe," Jean explained.

I ate the "Classique," consisting of egg, mushrooms, and cheese.

We left the port by car, and the landscape quickly changed from the sandy beaches of the Plage de Bordardoué to a coastline of tall cliffs and rock formations jutting from the water roughly one hundred feet into the air. The waves crashed against the rocks with a tremendous display of force and created a mist that dusted us at the top of the cliffs.

"This looks familiar, somehow," I told Odile as I studied the rock formations below.

"Those rock formations should be familiar. Claude Monet stayed here for two months and painted roughly forty works of art. Some of them, he painted right here at Port Coton. One of his famous works was called *The Needles of Port Coton*. You have undoubtedly seen his work at Jeu de Paume and many other museums in Paris. In fact, when Rodin saw the ocean off the coast of Vannes and on Belle-Île, he was heard to say, 'It's a Monet.'"

It was awe-inspiring to stand in the place where the father of Impressionism had painted some of his best works.

Our drive along the coast continued until the sky filled with bright streaks of orange and blue, and the sun disappeared behind the lighthouse. We returned to the Vannes harbor and enjoyed a dinner of "moules-frites," mussels with garlic, white wine and butter, and a side of fries. Walking alongside the medieval ramparts of the city was a perfect end to my weekend with a French family.

EASTER VACATION - APRIL 1979

Back in Paris, I watched the steam escape from the croissant as I pulled apart the layers, and the smell of melted butter filled my senses. The pastry paired perfectly with a café au lait, served in the traditional style—an empty coffee cup and two small pitchers, one filled with coffee and the other with steamed milk. Sunlight danced off the tulips in the café window as I studied my map of France.

"Eh, mec. Qu'est-ce que tu fais?" asked Pierre, the owner of the café.

I was his only customer at that moment, and he was eager to help me with my quest.

"I'm trying to decide where to go next weekend. Next Sunday is Easter, and I thought Heidi and I could get out and see something different."

"Have you ever been to Bayeux? It's right near the Normandy beaches of World War II and is home to the famous Bayeux Tapestry."

Pierre mapped out the route for us. Saturday morning, we would go through Pont-L'Évêque, Rouen, Trouville, and Bayeux. We would spend the night in Caen then drive back to Paris on Easter morning.

"Where should we stay in Caen?"

Pierre reassured me that there was no need to make reservations.

"There are plenty of hotels in Caen. It's not worth the trouble."

With Heidi's little red car stored safely in Switzerland for the year, she found a great deal on a rental car, and on Friday night, we packed our bags with the essentials—a baguette, cheese, wine, and grapes. We woke up extra early Saturday morning and were standing outside the car rental agency at seven o'clock when a man in a suit two sizes too small opened the door. After an extended time collecting paperwork, he walked us outside and gave us the keys to a nine-year-old faded-red Renault R4. It was a small four-door sedan that looked like it was part truck, part car. With 170,000 kilometers on the odometer, it was well-worn and ready for retirement. A cloud of smoke and a loud pop came out of the exhaust pipe, and we were on our way.

Traffic was heavy, and in two hours, we had made it only as far as Mantes-la-Jolie. Another pop came from the car, and the engine quit. Heidi managed to pull off the side of the road before it stopped completely. She turned the key. Nothing. Not a sound from the car. The gas gauge was still near full, but our Renault expressed no interest in taking a sip of petrol.

When I opened the hood, I was greeted by a tiny engine more fitting for a motorcycle than a car. All the spark plug cables looked tight, but the car still wouldn't start.

In desperation, I took out the crowbar.

"Don't hit it!" pleaded Heidi.

"Don't worry. I'm a professional. Sometimes, if you give everything a gentle tap, something will loosen up, and it'll start again."

I was actually stalling, hoping that after a rest, the engine would start.

After five minutes of me banging on the battery connections, the carburetor, and anything else I could see, Heidi turned the ignition switch, and Ole Red started right up. With the crowbar safely back under my seat, we headed through miles of farmland toward Rouen—Heidi and I, the master mechanic.

Place Saint-Marc bustled with activity as locals shopped the street markets for Easter. The scents of cheese, sausages, and fresh flowers surrounded us, and ladies with their carts discussed the weather while waiting their turn to select from a colorful array of cheeses in all shapes and sizes. On display were pistachio-encrusted goat cheese, Pont-L'Évêque (possibly the oldest cheese in France), Brie, Camembert, and Roquefort. Hundreds of vendors, most having a space no larger than ten by fifteen feet, sold everything from foie gras to fresh cider and from super-thick cream to barrels of butter. Up ahead was a market stall helmed by a skinny man with an overgrown white mustache and a captain's hat. At his table was a variety of Calvados, the local brandy made from Norman apples. After tasting a few samples, I settled on a small bottle of twenty-year-old "calva."

In the north of France, many people enjoyed a shot of calva between courses at dinnertime. This shot, called a "Trou Normand," or Norman hole, is said to help the diner make room for the next course by burning a hole through the previous courses in the stomachs of those who can get it down. At the nearby creperie, the Trou Normand sure helped me make room for the butter-sugar crepe I ate after enjoying the perfectly prepared crepe Breton with ham, cheese, and mushroom cream sauce I had for lunch.

An after-lunch walk among the half-timbered Norman buildings and the Rue du Gros-Horloge under the town clock brought us to the vieux marché, where Heidi pointed out a statue of Joan of Arc. The statue, only about six feet high, depicted a timid woman with short hair and a long robe, praying.

"She was burned at the stake right here, in 1431. Then they threw her ashes in the Seine."

Joan had led an army to victory roughly 530 years before the women's liberation movement took hold. Members of the clergy frowned upon her decision to wear men's clothes, even if it was to disguise her identity in the course of battle. She was convicted of cross-dressing and sentenced to death.

The two-hour drive to Bayeux was bumper to bumper all the way. We had no idea so many French wanted to be in Normandy for Easter.

"Deux audio-guides, en Français, s'il vous plait." Heidi asked the Bayeux Tapestry museum cashier for two headsets describing the tapestry in French.

The embroidered cloth was more than 220 feet long and was made in 1070, roughly 900 years before. Enclosed in glass, it wrapped around the edges of the museum hall. It was a bit like the world's longest comic strip, except that it described in pictures the Norman conquest of England. Replicas of the clothing, boats, and other artifacts depicted on the tapestry were also housed in the museum.

"Someone must have had a whole lot of time on their hands," I told Heidi after we returned our headsets and made our way to dinner.

The sun had set, and the roads were dark. Exhausted, we searched for a hotel. There was no way that either of us could drive what was certain to be a four- or five-hour trip back to Paris that night. But all the hotels in Bayeux were sold out. Heidi drove to Caen, a much larger city certain to have rooms. But hotel after hotel was full.

We stopped at the police station for advice.

"Everything has been sold out for weeks. It's Easter weekend."

Desperate and sleepy, we walked back to the car in the police station parking lot and fell asleep. The weather had cooled off quite a bit, and since we had no blankets or jackets, Heidi ran the car's heater every few minutes to keep us warm.

A policeman tapped on our window. "Shut off the car, or you'll die of carbon monoxide poisoning. Come inside the station, and you can sleep on the floor."

With just two drunks booked that night, only the bright lights, police radio, and concrete floor kept us from sleeping. But we were warm. At the first sign of sunrise, we returned the blankets borrowed from the police and were off to Paris.

The next evening, I stopped by the café on Glacière to thank Pierre for his advice. I asked him what he did for Easter.

"We stayed in Paris. With everyone out of town for the weekend, Paris was peaceful, and we enjoyed a pique-nique in the park."

A NIGHT AT THE OPERA

"Change into something nice. I want to take you somewhere tonight."

Without knowing where Heidi was taking me, I put on my best blue jeans and donned a pair of dress shoes. We exited the Metro at Opera. Heidi stopped at a kiosk and handed the man forty French francs, roughly six dollars, then showed me two tickets and said, "We're going to see Puccini's opera *La Bohème*, and I just got us last-minute tickets for twenty francs each."

She rushed me across the street.

"Do you see these two ramps? They were designed so that Napoleon III could safely enter and exit the theater in his carriage. There had been an assassination attempt at the old opera house, Salle Le Peletier, so Napoleon had this opera house built to be bigger and safer than the old one."

We handed the concierge our tickets and rushed up the grand staircase. Made of red and green marble and adorned with gold leaf and lit by torch-bearing marble statues, it was one of the most sumptuous works of art I had ever seen. Continuing up a few more levels, we finally arrived at a small balcony almost as high as the huge chandelier.

"Heidi, there are no chairs."

"True. At twenty francs, we have to stand. But we're here, and we can see *La Bohème*!"

I had never been to an opera before and had never heard of *La Bohème*—or Puccini for that matter. As far as I could tell, way down below, some tiny people were on stage singing in Italian while the backdrops changed, then everyone clapped and left their seats, except of course for us because we had no seats.

"Is it over?" I asked Heidi.

"No, it's just intermission. But did you see the chandelier? Isn't it beautiful? And it weighs almost fifteen thousand pounds."

"It is beautiful, but I would hate for it to fall. Someone could get hurt."

"Actually, in 1896, one of the counterweights fell and killed a concierge. It only missed Napoleon by twenty-three years!"

"Did you mean twenty-three feet?"

"No," said Heidi. "I meant twenty-three years. Napoleon died in 1873 without having seen a single performance at his new opera house."

With intermission over, we returned to our chairless balcony, feeling fortunate that we had seen more operas in the theater than the former emperor ever had.

ON MY OWN - MAY 1979

The reflection of a bright-orange sky painted the buildings on the east side of our courtyard as the sun set in the west. Children enjoyed their last few minutes of play before being called in for the night. I stared out our window, trying not to focus on the fact that tomorrow would be my last day of school. My coursework would be complete.

Heidi's voice broke through the silence. "Can you move the fondue pot and set the table for dinner?"

She was making some special Swiss dinner, but it wasn't fondue. The night before, it was beef fondue in hot oil, and earlier in the week, we'd had Emmentaler cheese fondue. I was just thinking about how unfond I was becoming of fondue when the pot briefly slipped from my hands. Some of the oil dripped onto the antique kitchen table that came with our furnished apartment. I tried to clean it up but made it even worse.

Heidi was too preoccupied to care as she set dinner on the table.

"It's Geschnetzeltes mit Rösti, veal in a brandy-and-white-wine mushroom-cream sauce served over shredded roasted potatoes."

As she flambéed the brandy, the aroma from the cream and wine filled the air, but my other senses were sending me warning signals. I was suspicious.

"You almost never cook. And now, this is the third night this week that you've made dinner. What's up?"

"I've got to return to Switzerland for six weeks of mandatory training in the Swiss Army. You can stay here, and I'll be back in June. My train leaves in the morning."

It took a moment for that to set in. I would be living alone in Paris. Now I understood why Heidi had insisted that I truly learn French. I remembered her saying something when she invited me to Paris about having to be gone for military training but had forgotten all about it. It was a difficult night. My feelings for Heidi were growing stronger, and she was leaving. Maybe I would tell her the next day before she left.

The next morning, just as on my previous visits to the station, there I was, saying goodbye to a good friend. I almost said something to Heidi about my feelings for her, but the station was chaotic, and Heidi was running late. As the train pulled away, she looked out the window and tried to cheer me up by crossing her eyes, sticking her tongue out, and wiggling her fingers behind her ears. I smiled then walked slowly, head down, trying to muster the courage to live in Paris on my own. At the 8 à Huit, Popeye stopped to visit for a few minutes with Caroline. We explained to both Caroline and Marie-Thérèse that Heidi would be gone for six weeks and that I would be on my own. Marie-Therese offered to help if I needed anything during that time.

The last day of school was bittersweet. Many of the students I knew were returning to their home countries. Adel was going back to Iran (possibly to finish the revolution), Demetri to Greece, and Petra to Germany. Others would stay on and take advanced courses.

A cloud of cigarette smoke greeted me as I opened the door to Petra's apartment that evening. She was hosting a party for all of us students before leaving the next day. Conversations flowed as freely as the rum from the bottle we passed around the room. As the clock passed 2 a.m., we hugged each other and said goodbye, knowing it was unlikely we would ever see each other again. At least I could be content knowing that I was staying in Paris.

Students from French class, Paris 1979

The next morning, the sun warmed my table outside La
Contrescarpe, but somehow, I still felt cold. The café on the
south side of the Place de la Contrescarpe was a good goto restaurant when I needed a change from my local haunts.
On that day, however, no amount of confiture could make
my croissant seem sweet. School was over, Heidi was back
in Switzerland, and I felt truly alone. Furthermore, I was
down to my last two hundred dollars, some of which was
needed for my Carte Orange, the monthly Metro/bus pass.
That coffee and croissant would be my last meal out for
quite a while.

Paris toyed with my emotions as I walked along the
banks of the Seine. Lovers walked hand in hand on Île-
Saint-Louis. The roses behind Notre Dame were the most

vibrant red I had ever seen, and only one wispy cloud unsuccessfully attempted to cast darkness onto the day. But still, somehow, I felt as if Paris had abandoned me. In reality, she was preparing me for the next stage of our love affair. She was drawing me in. It was time to find a job—to find permanent employment in France.

GETTING A JOB - MAY 1979

As the train left Gare Saint-Lazare, I wondered what it would be like to take that train to work every day. Dosapro Milton Roy in Pont-Saint-Pierre was almost two hours from Paris, but it was the only job lead I had in France. As a foreigner, I couldn't simply walk into an office and fill out an application for employment. I would need a work visa, and few employers would be interested in working through the bureaucratic process of helping me obtain one. But Thierry Lepage, the responsable de l'informatique (IT manager) at Dosapro, remembered me from Florida. On the phone a week earlier, he'd sounded eager to see me and make good on his year-old promise to offer me a job.

Passing Giverny, I allowed my thoughts to drift to Claude Monet, who years earlier had created masterpieces in the gardens outside his home. But my stomach was more concerned with food than with Monet's water lilies. With money running low, I had skipped breakfast and had eaten only a can of ratatouille for dinner the night before.

The scenery changed from the suburbs of Paris to

rolling hills, green pastures, and an occasional forest as the train entered Normandy. Seeing the cows enjoying their hay reminded me of my own hunger. I came up with a plan—Popeye! My trusted puppet friend came to life immediately after I pulled him out of my backpack and placed him on my hand. I moved to the dining car.

"Je suis ce que je suis," Popeye said, entertaining the diners. "Does anyone have spinach? I need spinach."

No one had spinach, but Popeye collected two rolls and one croissant. Popeye and I returned to our seats and enjoyed our newfound treasure. As sad as it was that I had to beg for food, salvation was less than an hour away in Pont-Saint-Pierre.

Popeye had just been tucked away in my backpack when Thierry greeted me at the platform, offering me a firm handshake and a ride from the train station to Dosapro Milton Roy. The factory was more like a collection of old farmhouses than a pump-manufacturing plant. Fish were plentiful in the Andelle river, which flowed through the property, and a fish market was within walking distance of the building. I would enjoy working there, I thought, even though the daily commute would be long.

Thierry gave me a tour of the facility then took me to the personnel office. My months of education in French paid off as I easily answered the questions of the Human Relations lady before Thierry and I settled in his office to discuss the latest programming techniques. But I still had one question stemming from my visit to Personnel. "Thierry, why did she have me sign a blank sheet of paper?"

He laughed. "That's for your signature analysis. It's a standard part of the interview process here. You might be surprised what you can learn about someone just from their signature."

I was thinking about how I had rushed through the signature and wondered what that might indicate when a loud bell pierced the air. The assembly-line workers shut off their equipment and joined each other in the cafeteria for lunch. Thierry took me to a local bistro.

He exchanged pleasantries with the waitress, who promptly sat us at a table in the back of the dining room. She set two half-full glasses of water directly in front of me. Her round face and brown eyes were a close match to that of the older woman with the food-stained apron who was looking out at us from the kitchen. While menus were located by the door, they hadn't been offered to us. Only a glass of red wine for Thierry and the two half-glasses of water for me.

I had reached for the water when Thierry put his hand over my glass. "Attendez."

Ever more curious, I waited. He poured the contents of one water glass into the other, turning the mixture chalky white. A nod indicated that it was now okay for me to take a drink. Staring at the results of his magic trick in a glass, I had suddenly lost my thirst. But Thierry implored me to drink, so I grabbed the glass and took a large gulp. The alcohol hit my tongue first, followed by the strong flavor of black licorice. I winced as I swallowed, looking up to see Thierry smiling.

"Anisette," he explained.

Just then, twelve dead snails immersed in melted butter appeared in front of me. At least those, I recognized— escargot. In my Florida family, dead snails were not part of our culinary traditions. Thinking that the rubbery-looking creatures wanted to go back into their shells, I noticed Thierry waiting for me to dig in.

The first bite had the texture of a soft earthy meat. The flavor was balanced perfectly by the melted butter, and the delicate aroma of garlic delighted my nose. Those escargots were so tasty, I almost forgot about the anisette.

Thierry's face turned serious as he made space on the paper tablecloth. He drew five squares.

"These are the five programmers you met this morning. Due to budget cuts, three of them will be laid off next week."

He drew x's over three of the squares. I saw where the conversation was going.

"So, unfortunately, we won't be able to hire you. I'm so sorry."

Stunned, I looked away and wondered what to do next. Where would I go? I didn't even have enough money left to return to Florida.

Thierry continued, "I ran you through the interview with our personnel department this morning to give you a chance to get acquainted with the hiring process here in France. So, while it's true that we can't hire you here at Dosapro Milton Roy, I have friends in my data processing club who are looking for developers. And since experienced software developers are rare in France, employers are willing to work with the authorities to get you a work visa quickly. Here's a list I've compiled for you."

From his notebook, he pulled out a typewritten list of three companies, all in the Paris area.

"And so you don't show up empty-handed, I've also prepared this."

He handed me a handwritten page that read:

Dear Friends,

I met Monsieur Frangipane when he was working for our American division in Florida. He displayed exceptional design and programming skills while creating their order entry system. If you need a programmer, I highly recommend him.

Thierry Lepage

I placed the two valuable items in my inner coat pocket. Still, I said nothing, wondering whether his note would truly help.

"Let's go for a walk," he said, standing up and heading toward the door.

"But what about the bill?" I asked.

Thierry laughed. As we walked out the door, he explained, "The woman in the kitchen? That's my sister. She and her husband own this little bistro. And they're teaching my niece the business as well."

While walking through the country roads of Pont-Saint-Pierre, Thierry gave me tips to prepare for interviews with other companies.

"Don't ask about money. That will come at the end. Oh, and don't use Franglais. Speak pure French whenever possible."

By the time we finished our walk, we had discussed my life in France and his experiences in the United States and compared the two. As we arrived at the office, the bells were sounding again on the assembly line—that time indicating the end of the workday. Just like at midday, the workers shut off their equipment and headed toward the door. But three of them reached into a closet and grabbed fishing poles. Seeing my interest, Thierry walked me out back, along the banks of the Andelle.

"They are catching their dinner," he said.

The men now sitting on the river's edge nodded.

During the long, lonely ride back to Paris, I sat in my seat, staring at the two notes from Thierry that were in my lap.

While I was confident in my programming skills, my fear at having to go through more job interviews in French was intense. "I can do this," I thought, attempting to convince myself.

The first company on the list was Logabax in Arcueil, a city roughly thirty minutes south of Paris. I would call in the morning to try to set up an appointment. That night, over a dinner of peanut butter and jelly on a baguette, I studied the map, planning a route.

THE FIRST FRENCH PERSONAL COMPUTER

"Demain matin à neuf heures. Au revoir, Monsieur Frangipane."

Jean-Pierre Rouart from Logabax had agreed to speak with me the following morning at his office on Rue Aristide Briand in Arcueil. He explained that Logabax was a new company, producing the first French personal computer.

The bus to Denfert-Rochereau, then the Metro to Arcueil, a ten-minute walk to Rue Aristide Briand, and I was staring at a sign reading simply, "Logabax Informatique."

While the receptionist went to find Jean-Pierre, I looked over the lobby. "The First French Personal Computer," a sign proudly boasted in English. A poster behind the receptionist's desk showed a dog lying next to a keyboard. "Friendly," it proclaimed in my mother tongue.

"Monsieur Frangipane?"

Startled, I turned around.

"Bonjour. My name is Jean-Pierre Rouart."

He walked me into his office. "Please sit down. You come highly recommended," Jean-Pierre said, leaning back in his desk chair. "Do you know Basic?"

After more than an hour of discussing various programming languages and operating systems, he told me that I was just what he needed.

"We need you to write a free-form database for use at SICOB in Paris this fall. It will showcase our products. The SICOB computer show has been around since 1950, and this year, Valéry Giscard d'Estaing, the president of France, will give the keynote speech, so this is an important year for us at the show. Follow me. Here's where you'll be working."

Two metal desks, two wooden chairs, one bookshelf, and barren walls were the only things in my austere future office.

"Will I have my own computer?" I asked.

"Well, yes, but we're a little short on them right now." Jean-Pierre looked at the floor as he spoke. "But there is one in another office. Let me show you."

A short walk down the hall took us to a table holding one computer monitor, a keyboard, and a computer resembling a huge toaster with two floppy disk drives. Looking closely at the monitor, I could see the "Hazeltine" logo from New York. Jean-Pierre proudly lifted the cover off the computer. On the inside were the floppy disk drives made in the USA by Shugart, and the chips depicted the outline of Texas, clearly made by Texas Instruments. As he closed the cover, he looked at me and asked, "Did I mention that we're the first French personal computer company?"

Back in Jean-Pierre's office, we discussed my salary. To be sure I understood clearly, he wrote as he spoke.

"Your salary will be five thousand French francs per month." He wrote:

5000 x 13 = 65.000 FF

"So that comes to sixty-five thousand French francs annually."

I stared at the 13 on the page, thought a bit, and said, "In my country, we only have twelve months."

Jean-Pierre laughed. "Yes, but in France, you get the entire month of August off for vacation."

Looking more confused than ever, I said nothing.

"Since August is your vacation, you receive two months' pay instead of one. Otherwise, how would you pay for your time at the beach?"

"How indeed?" I thought.

Jean-Pierre's face turned serious again.

"Since you don't have a working visa yet, for now, we can't hire you."

My heart sank.

The process of obtaining a work visa could take months, and I was out of money. My mind raced.

Then Jean-Pierre continued his explanation. "Until then, you'll be paid as an outside consultant. Set up a bank account at a Swiss bank that also has a branch here in Paris. We'll send your payment to Switzerland, and you can withdraw it right here in Paris. I'll work on processing your work visa. You should have it in six short months or so."

After a firm handshake, I found my way back to the Metro station, now an employed programmer in Paris!

Reflecting on the day's events while on the return trip home, I thought, "Alice in Wonderland, you've got nothing on me. I work for a French computer manufacturing company where seemingly everything is made in the United States. My company has thirteen months in a year yet only one computer, and I am now a Swiss consultant, about to have my first Swiss bank account."

Back at the apartment, I did my best over a poor phone

connection to tell Heidi the news. Then reality set in. I didn't even have enough money to get to Switzerland to open the required bank account.

Heidi reminded me, "I'm still employed by Societé Banque Suisse. I'll go into the bank tomorrow and set up your account. Congratulations on the job!"

As I headed off to sleep, the intrigue of foreign bank accounts faded, and I focused on my new long-term life in France. With my monthly salary at roughly $1,250 US dollars per month and our total rent at $350 US dollars per month, I could support myself comfortably and pay half the rent.

How many years would I stay? How would my parents take the news? Would I be in Paris for life?

LE TRAVAIL - JUNE 1979

Over time, I adjusted to the work life in Paris. A short walk to the bus, then the Metro to Arcueil, and finally a short walk to Logabax. I worked on my database program, waiting until one of our two computers in the office became available for me to test. After seven and a half hours of work each day, I returned to Paris, picked up a demi-baguette to go with dinner, and relaxed at the apartment.

A few weeks later, I thought about my new life as the Metro sped toward my place of employment. Then, in the darkness of the tunnel between stations, the train came to a complete stop. A few minutes passed before the conductor's voice was heard over the speakers.

"We are having a thirty-minute transit strike and will resume our normal schedule when the strike is over." The doors opened, providing welcome relief from the heat.

Strikes over health benefits, vacation time, or schedules were common in Paris, and the other passengers weren't at all bothered that we were stuck somewhere underground at the mercy of the conductor. While I stared out the window, hoping that any trains behind us were also on strike, the other passengers continued to read the latest issues of *Le Monde* and *Le Figaro* as if nothing was amiss. After we spent half an hour in the tunnel, the doors shut, and the train completed its journey with no further announcements from the conductor.

Jean-Pierre wanted to see how my work was coming along. With the SICOB computer show coming in September, it was important that I be making progress, especially since the company would shut down for the month of August. I proudly showed him what I had completed, but a disappointed look crossed his face.

"Barry, I must explain something to you. We sell quite a few computers to the French government, and they don't allow the use of Franglais in our software."

I knew all about "Franglais," the use of English words in French sentences. My coworkers used the English "computer," even though the French word "ordinateur" had the same meaning. But when I was writing software, commonly used words like "computer," "database," and "software" had to be replaced with "ordinateur," "base de donneés," and "logiciel."

After explaining the requirements, Jean-Pierre looked at me and in English said, "Okay?"

I dared not respond with "okay" in English but used the French equivalent. "D'accord," I replied.

Now gainfully employed, I enjoyed a plate of steak frites at a local brasserie before heading home. Heidi would return from Switzerland soon, and I wanted the apartment to be clean and tidy. As a reminder of the hard times in my recent past, I left my last remaining can of ratatouille on the kitchen counter.

HEIDI'S RETURN - JUNE 1979

After adjusting to living alone, I was excited to have my friend back from Switzerland. She returned to Paris late on a Friday night, long after I had gone to sleep. But the next morning, I woke up early to get fresh croissants for the two of us.

"Bonjour, monsieur."

The lady greeted me in the usual fashion at our local boulangerie.

As I started my request of "deux croissants, s'il vous plait," I heard, "No, no. Open the door, monsieur!"

A small bird had followed me into the tiny store, and it was frantically flying around, trying to find its way out. It flew from the croissants to the pastries and even perched on top of a baguette before being coaxed outside while I held the door open. Most of the pastries were ruined, as the frightened bird had relieved itself when it flew into the glass case. As quickly as possible, I purchased an undamaged baguette and left the store.

Heidi was in the kitchen when I returned.

"Good morning, sweetie. Did anything come in the mail while I was in Switzerland?"

"Nope, just the usual advertisements. And no visa."

Interesting. Heidi had never called me "sweetie" before.

We were both eager to get back into our normal Parisian life. Over a breakfast of bread and confiture, we discussed the day's excursions. She selected Musée Marmottan and Memorial des Martyrs de la Déportation, two museums I had never heard of.

Travel guidebooks, in their desire to tell us what to see, by omission wind up telling us what *not* to see as well. For me, having a guidebook tell me what to visit in a city would be like having a stranger explain what I should enjoy about a new girlfriend. Some things are best experienced on our own, each of us deciding what is most important about a person or a place.

At the edge of Bois de Boulogne, Musée Marmottan was a place like this. Barely mentioned in the guidebooks, it was a museum dedicated almost exclusively to the life of Claude Monet. Containing personal letters of the artist and nearly one hundred paintings of his including a small piece entitled *Impression, Sunrise* (which gave the Impressionist movement its name in 1874), the museum was a sheer delight without the crowds of the Louvre. It was amazing how such a priceless work of art could be approached, likely even touched, without any visible protection. The impression of light reflecting off the water and of the sunrise over the harbor of Le Havre truly changed the direction of modern art, moving away from dark paintings of fruit and dead animals to a new world of bright colors and movement. While the painting contained nothing other than rough brush strokes, I could almost hear the water lapping on the edge of the boats and feel the heat from the sun as it rose over the harbor, even though a thick haze obscured most of the sky. Captivated by the complexities in the simple painting, I stood still, listening to what the brush strokes had to say. After a long visit, we left the Musée Marmottan and took the Metro to Notre Dame.

Hiding underground behind Notre Dame was the Memorial des Martyrs de la Déportation, a little-known memorial to the French exterminated by the Nazis in World War II. It provided a stark contrast to the merriment of the tourists above ground.

After descending the stairway from the rose garden, we came upon a window overlooking the river Seine. As if inside a prison, the window had iron bars. Looking between the bars, we could see barges moving downstream. The contrast between the free-flowing river and the iron bars tugged at my heart.

A narrow corridor forced us, along with the other visitors, into a single-file line, and we exited into a dark room facing a prison cell with more iron bars. All noise of

Paris disappeared, replaced by a deafening silence as the weight of the exhibit became apparent. The walls of the cell were filled with 200,000 tiny lights, each representing a soul deported and killed during the occupation. Two hundred thousand people had lost their lives simply for belonging to a particular religion—for being Jews. It was all too easy for leaders in Germany at the time to blame the country's ills on a particular segment of society, stirring up a frenzy leading to the demise of innocents.

The memorial was created in 1952, serving as a reminder of the atrocities and asking us to forgive but never forget.

A Frenchman turned to me and asked, "What will prevent this from happening again today, with another religion in another land?"

I had no response to a very good question.

From the frenzy of the bird in the boulangerie to the beauty of Claude Monet's family museum to the sobriety of the Memorial des Martyrs de la Déportation, Paris continued to provide me with life lessons, some more significant than others.

MONTMARTRE

"Allo, taxi?" I answered the phone at home in the usual way, but that time, it was just Claude, the concierge of the apartment.

"You have mail today, Monsieur Frangipane."

Hoping that my visa had arrived, I ran downstairs to find only an envelope from Logabax with copies of my work visa application, along with the usual advertisements. While it was good to see that things were moving along, I was getting nervous about not having my actual work visa. Before long, I would reach the six-month mark in France, and without a visa, I would need to visit some other fine country, once again in search of a passport stamp.

Disappointed, I placed the visa application papers back in the envelope and put it in my folder marked "Important Papers."

"Was that everything in today's mail?" Heidi asked.

"That was it. No visa today."

"Why don't you go up to Montmartre?" she suggested. "The walk up the hill will be good for you. But be careful. In 250 AD, Saint Denis lost his head up there."

Lost his head, indeed. He was decapitated for preaching Christianity, and the hill was named "Hill of the martyr" or Montmartre after this headless man.

The walk from the Metro stop Anvers up two hundred steps to the Sacre Coeur on top of Montmartre rewarded me with panoramic views of the city—a flat landscape of six-story buildings punctuated by a few churches, Montparnasse Tower, and the Eiffel Tower. Montmartre was once the home to masters such as Renoir, Van Gogh, Monet, and Sisley. Even on that afternoon, I could see local artists having lunch in the smaller bistros while discussing their work. Some of the younger ones still had their dreams ahead of them, while the elders seemed resigned to a life of

Sacre Cœur, Montmartre

haggling with tourists, in multiple languages, over the price of a painting of La Tour Eiffel they had recreated hundreds of times.

At Place du Tertre, the square where painters have displayed their work for centuries, artists appeared to be just finishing their latest masterpieces. That was no coincidence. A French friend had explained that they were using a textured process called silk-screening where a painting is duplicated in a factory, and the "artist" adds a bit of paint so the tourist will think it's an original.

"Most," he explained, "are true artists, and their work is quite good. They brave the biting cold winds and rain on the top of Montmartre to make a living. It's bad for their health, but passion for their work drives them to stay."

One artist had a few large paintings of farmhouses and fields in the style of the Impressionists. The contrast between the light yellow of the wheat fields and the azure sky was so stunning that I decided to take a picture of his painting. I knelt and, carefully focusing, took a great photograph of his best work. As I got up off my knees and walked away, satisfied with my shot, I heard someone yelling behind me. It was the artist, chasing me across the square. I ran through the crowd and ducked into a souvenir shop, hiding behind the scarves and umbrellas. Maybe taking photos of an artist's work wasn't such a good idea. Heidi was right. A guy could lose his head.

Dreams Change

AU REVOIR, MA CHERIE - JUNE 1979

Heidi appeared especially pensive as we enjoyed our croissants and café au lait, gazing out our windows at the morning activities in our courtyard.

"Barry, I received a phone call yesterday from my bank. They told me to return to work, so I'll be cutting short my studies at the Sorbonne and returning to Zurich in August."

"When will you be returning to Paris?"

"I don't know. They're giving me a new position, so I don't anticipate returning to Paris except for vacation."

"But what about the apartment?"

Heidi pulled out a scratch pad and started writing. "Look, with your job, based on my calculations, you can continue to rent the apartment on your own. It'll be tighter for you, certainly, but you can always look for a smaller place in the future, or maybe Logabax will give you a raise. Let's go for a walk and talk about it."

The numbers she had written were no consolation for the fact that I would now be truly on my own in Paris. The flowers of Parc Montsouris were in full bloom in late June as if to reassure me that my life in Paris would be rosy.

Heidi walked with me to the top of the hill overlooking the park.

"Don't worry. With a great job, an apartment, and a good handle on the language, you're all set to succeed."

My heart sank. I concluded from her words that she was not nearly as interested in me as I was in her. Maybe it was the age difference. I couldn't be sure. But I said nothing. It was too late.

The sun's reflection across the lake was disturbed by a family of ducks paddling across the center. I thought about my future. Would I find someone, get married, and stay in Paris? Would we then, like the ducks, visit the park with our children? Why couldn't it be Heidi? Or would Paris have something else in store for my future?

The street market along Boulevard Auguste Blanqui was busy as we meandered toward our apartment, neither of us wanting to rush home. Foie gras, truffle-infused sausages, goat cheese covered in pistachios, and fresh roasted chickens were among the morning's choices. Older couples shopped together, one selecting merchandise while the other slowly counted out the coins needed for the purchase. I wondered if that was my future—years of going to the market every day with my wife, enjoying everything Paris had to offer.

While my ability to speak and understand French had improved, the idea of living in Paris without Heidi was no longer appealing. We had only one month left together in Paris. One month before I was truly on my own.

LEAVING WORK - JULY 1979

Over the previous few weeks, I had taken on a secret project for work. Having taken to heart Jean-Pierre's comments about Franglais, I decided to write the first Basic interpreter written entirely in French. With this tool, the programmers at Logabax would be able to use French words when writing programs. "GOTO" became "ALLEZ." "STOP" translated to "ARRETEZ." After checking my work carefully, I made copies for Jean-Pierre. Excited about my project, I explained it to another employee. He liked the work I showed him but asked, "Excuse me, you have a bit of an accent. What part of France are you from?"

The question floored me. I was no longer being seen as a foreigner but rather as someone from a different part of France. From a language standpoint at least, I had made it. Delighted and with copies of my work in hand, I walked into Jean-Pierre's office.

"Jean-Pierre, I have something special to show you. Can we go into the room with the computer so I can demonstrate?"

Dreams Change

At the computer, I slid my diskette into the slot and turned on the machine.

"Look, a Basic interpreter in French!"

I proudly showed my boss how I had changed "IF" to "SI," "END" to "FIN," and all the other translations. "You see, now the French programmers will have an easier time writing programs, and there's no English!"

Jean-Pierre had been listening quietly, waiting for me to finish.

"This is very good work, but I'm afraid that the standard for Basic is English. It's what everyone knows. We really don't need it in French. Even though the French government will not permit English to be displayed on the screen, the programming languages themselves are not in question."

Sitting in silence, thinking about all those nights I had worked on the project, I barely heard his next few sentences.

"There's been a hiring freeze. We haven't been able to produce many computers, so sales have been very slow. We won't be able to hire anyone else until next year."

While disappointed to hear of the slumping sales, I wasn't quite sure why he was explaining all of that to me. But then he continued.

"And since technically you aren't an employee, when we close for August, you won't be able to return to work in September. So July 31 will be your last day."

That, I understood.

Heidi was leaving at the end of July, and so was my job. Knowing that Heidi would soon be gone, I didn't have the emotional energy needed to search for another job. My time in France was coming to an end. Paris was sending me home.

8 À HUIT

A few days had passed when Daniel from 8 à Huit saw me walking to the boulangerie for my morning croissants.

"I just heard the news yesterday. Caroline told us that you're leaving. Since you aren't working today, why don't you come to the wholesale market in Rungis with me this morning? I've got to get food for the store."

We hopped into his three-wheeled enclosed van. The tiny engine and the chassis competed to see which could make the most noise as we sped toward the south of Paris at a brisk forty miles per hour. Daniel yelled as he drove.

"The food market used to be in Les Halles, right in the center of Paris. But it was only twenty acres, way too small to service the entire city. So ten years ago, it was moved to Rungis, where it has grown to almost six hundred acres."

Daniel navigated his minivan into the center of the massive complex. One section had cattle in various states of undress hanging from large meat hooks. Next, there were tables of fish as far as I could see. Buyers and sellers moved at a frenetic pace.

"This place is huge!" I told Daniel.

He briefly paused from loading vegetables into the van and smiled. "Yes, they say that the market is larger than the entire principality of Monaco. Almost everything you eat in Paris, from the largest restaurants to small stores like ours, comes from here. They open at 1 a.m. and close before midday. This gives buyers time to restock while their stores and restaurants are closed."

After about an hour in this unending city of food, we made one final stop in the cheese suburb before heading back to 8 à Huit. Daniel invited Heidi and me to join his family at a local restaurant that evening. He confided that his family was quite sad that we were leaving.

While dining with our friends, we learned that Daniel spoke fairly good English, as he had spent a few years visiting his brother, who lived in Canada. He was too shy to use his English with us, and that was why we didn't know he spoke it, Marie-Thérèse explained.

I invited the family to visit me in Florida whenever they wanted. Caroline gave me a picture she had drawn of Heidi and me on the curb outside the store. Heidi, in return, gave her a one-pound bar of Toblerone direct from Switzerland.

LEAVING HOME - JULY 1979

With only a week left before our departure, our landlord, Nicole, stopped by during the afternoon for a semifinal inspection of the apartment. I had packed almost everything and taken many items out to the trash bin. There was my plastic washing machine, containers of spices, and even the last can of ratatouille I was saving as a memory of my hard times. They weren't just household items being thrown away; they were to be the beginnings of my new life in Paris. My copy of *Le Petit Nicolas,* which Heidi had given me, went into my suitcase as a memory of the dream that almost came true.

Nicole rang the intercom buzzer precisely at 1 p.m. Heidi and I made one last walk through the rooms while our landlord made her way up to our floor.

She was thorough with her inspection, checking the plumbing, the hot plates, our rotisserie oven, and even sitting in the chairs to be certain none of them were broken. As she was giving us our final instructions, her eyes focused on the antique table upon which we had spilled fondue oil months earlier.

"Mon Dieu, la table! What did you do to my table?"

Heidi stammered, "There was a small incident with the fondue pot."

"Well, that table will need to be refinished, or it will come out of the deposit. I will see you two next week for the final inspection!"

As the sound of her footsteps down the stairs became faint, I looked at the table and compared the part with the fondue oil with the original undamaged area.

"Hey, Heidi, I think I know what we can do with the table."

"It's too late. No one will be able to refinish it in the week we have left. She'll just have to take the money out of our deposit."

"No, wait. The part with the vegetable oil looks better than the original. Let me cover the entire table with vegetable oil, work it in, then dry it off with paper towels. What do we have to lose?"

I ran down to the 8 à Huit for a fresh bottle of sunflower oil and a roll of paper towels. Nothing but the best would do for my woodworking project. Heidi laughed as she watched me carefully distribute the contents of my homemade restoration kit on the table's surface. Working the oil evenly into the wood was giving it a richer look, but it took a few applications over the week to complete the task. Wiping off the last telltale signs of our efforts, I realized my work was done.

Heidi looked impressed. "Nice work. We just might pull this off."

Nicole returned for the final inspection and checked first on her priceless table. She looked astonished as she analyzed the surface.

"It looks beautiful again! What did you use to restore the finish?"

"It was simple. We just—"

Heidi interrupted me. "We just used a special oil product… my brother sent me from Switzerland."

"That's amazing! What's the name of this product?"

Heidi and I looked at each other.

"I'll get the name of it from my brother and send it to you when I get back to Zurich."

LE DÉPART - JULY 31, 1979

I woke up early and walked my beloved Paris on my own. After a pain au chocolat from our local boulangerie, I walked down Rue Mouffetard and ended up at Notre Dame. The time had passed so quickly. It seemed like only a few weeks earlier that I had been standing outside the doors of the cathedral, waiting for my friend to arrive and for my adventure to begin. Now it was ending abruptly. Sure, my visit was only intended to last for a year, but I had hoped for, I had *wanted* so much more. "Was it just a silly dream to expect the adventure to continue?" I asked myself. Sitting on the banks of the Seine, I watched my reflection in the water come and go with the ripples in the river. It was time to face reality. Time to go back to the apartment, grab our bags, and leave.

Heidi and I stopped outside Luxembourg Gardens for one final egg-cheese-and-oregano crepe before boarding the Metro to the train station. After taking one last look at Gare de l'Est, we settled in our seats on the train to Switzerland. We would travel to Zurich together and spend a week at her parents' house outside the city, then I would return to Florida.

Theirs was a small but efficient home on a hillside overlooking Lake Zurich, surrounded by gardens and trees. Heidi's mother was a petite, quiet Philippine woman with long black hair who hugged me and told me how happy she was to have me stay at their home. Her father, however, a tall, stern Swiss-German, was far more interested in the date of my departure than the date of my arrival. He begrudgingly shook my hand before returning to reading the newspaper.

The next day, Heidi's mother prepared a lunch including fresh tomatoes and lettuce from their garden and invited us all to eat outside on the picnic table in the shade of a large cherry tree. "As a special treat for our guest, I have prepared cow tongue as our main course."

Sure enough, there it was in all its glory—a cow tongue on my plate as if it had just been cut out of the cow's mouth and placed carefully in front of me. I took one bite and stopped eating.

"Mom," Heidi explained, "they don't eat a lot of tongue in the United States, so I'm not sure Barry likes it."

Heidi's father rolled his eyes and said something to Heidi in German. Later, I asked her what he'd said.

"He said that house guests are like fresh fish. After a few days, they begin to stink."

That day, August 1, was Swiss National Day.

"Let's climb up into the tree," suggested Heidi. "It's the first night of August, and to celebrate, everyone on the hillside starts a bonfire. The entire valley lights up as far as you can see."

We climbed up the tree and ate cherries as the bonfires appeared across the valley. Bittersweet emotions filled my head while we enjoyed our last evening together. In a few days, Heidi would start her new position at the bank in Zurich, and I would look for work in Florida.

LOST IN LONDON

The following afternoon, I prepared my bags for the overnight train to London and the flight from London to Florida. My remaining cash was used for the train ticket, and Heidi gave me something called a EuroCheque to purchase my plane ticket in London.

"It's as good as cash," she said before driving me to the Zurich train station as she had a few years prior during my first-ever trip to Europe.

After a sad goodbye with my friend, I boarded the train. From my carriage window, I waved and made funny faces at Heidi.

As the train pulled away, she said, "Goodbye, sweetie," and continued to wave until she was out of sight.

I wondered if we would ever see each other again. I wanted to tell her I loved her, but first, there was the age difference as well as my being afraid of telling her I loved her in French. Mostly, perhaps, I feared she might not feel the same way.

Settled in my couchette, I closed my eyes, thinking about what might have been. I slept until the next morning, when the train stopped in Calais, France. In the port of Calais, everyone got off the train and walked onto a ferry for the trip across the English Channel. During the brief crossing, I met the former British ambassador to Australia, who delighted in showing me how the slot machines worked on the ferry.

Dreams Change

"You just put one French franc in the slot, press the button, and… Darn it, I lost."

Having only about forty francs left to my name, I was hardly interested in his losing proposition. But to humor my new friend, I inserted one franc and pushed the button as he had instructed me. To my surprise, roughly fifty francs came out, more than doubling my net worth. My friend grumbled and returned to his seat.

Once I was off the ferry, the train took me to London, where I rushed to the downtown airline ticket counter.

"You've purchased the last seat on the flight," the agent said as she took my EuroCheque. "Wait. Who is Heidi? If this isn't your check, you can't use it to pay for your ticket."

Pleading with the agent, I explained that I had no money for a hotel and only the equivalent of about fifteen dollars in cash.

"I'll hold the ticket for you for three hours while you sort out your finances. It's the best I can do. You can leave your bags here in the office if you want."

Alone and afraid, I walked out of the office with nowhere in particular to go. That was not how I'd expected my Parisian adventure to end. But there I was in London with no money, no place to stay, and no way to get back to Florida. Sitting on a park bench across town, I flipped through my wallet, partly to look at photos of my family and partly to look for phone numbers or ideas about what to do next. Then I saw it. Tucked away in a hidden flap of my wallet was a Mastercard I had acquired while still employed in Florida. I had never used it, and it hadn't expired but had only a three-hundred-dollar credit limit. Two hours had already passed when I rushed across town to get back to the ticketing agent. The credit card covered the two-hundred-fifty-dollar plane ticket, and I was on my way home.

A wave of emotions hit me during takeoff. I had left home to live in Paris, learn the language, and get a job, and I had accomplished all of those things. But there was so much more to do. What had happened that sent Heidi back to Switzerland so soon? I'd thought we would be there the entire year. And why did I wait so long to tell Heidi how I felt about her? Or more accurately, why didn't I ever get up the courage to share my feelings? What if I had? Would it have changed anything?

Seeing me sobbing in my seat, the lady sitting next to me asked if I was okay.

"Yes, I'm okay. I'm going home."

THE TEASE - OCTOBER 1979

Months passed, and my life back in the Sunshine State resumed. Mom and Dad were making preparations for Christmas. I had found another job as a computer programmer and tried my best to fit in. But I had been forever changed by Paris in my seven-month immersion there. Even speaking English wasn't as easy as it once was. "How do you say so-and-so in English?" I asked frequently, finding myself thinking in French and mentally translating back to English before speaking.

After dinner, as part of his daily ritual, my father went through the day's mail. "You have a letter from France."

He handed it to me then continued to thumb through the rest, separating the bills from the junk. I rushed to open the envelope. It had been mailed to my old Paris address and took almost three months to get to me in Florida. The letter read simply:

Dear Barry,

Our hiring freeze has ended, and your work visa has come through. Would you be interested in returning to Logabax?

Sincerely,

Jean-Pierre Rouart

Logabax Informatique

I placed the letter on the coffee table next to *Le Petit Nicolas* and stared out the window, thinking. My work visa had finally arrived. But I was now firmly back in the States, with a good job and surrounded by family and friends. Though his offer was enticing, I couldn't bear the thought of returning to life in Paris without Heidi. The pain of the abrupt ending was still too strong, and it was too soon. The letter went back into its envelope as if to finish the chapter of my life in Paris.

I closed my eyes and dozed off in the chair, wanting to hear Heidi call me "sweetie" one more time.

The Occasional Visitor

Life back in Florida became the norm, but somehow, I no longer fit in. My heart was still with Paris and my former "roommate."

———— ◆ ————

A NEW GENERATION - 1981-1987

Correspondence with Heidi became less and less frequent. I kept my emotions to myself, and her letters started to feel a bit short and lacking in feeling. We completely lost touch after I married in 1981. Over time, my wife and I had two daughters, Stephanie and Amber. In the early '80s, the closest I came to Paris was the EPCOT center at Walt Disney World in Orlando, where the French pavilion showed the eighteen-minute movie *Impressions de France*, highlighting Notre Dame, the Eiffel Tower, the markets in Normandy, pastries in Paris, and hot-air ballooning over the Loire Valley from the Château de Chaumont. I must have watched that movie over a hundred times, wishing I was back in Paris. As my income grew, we were able to save money for an annual trip to France by postponing the purchase of a new car and doing whatever else was necessary. I was fortunate that my job as a computer programmer gave me frequent flyer points that I could use for plane tickets.

On our first family trip to Paris, we went to Luxembourg Gardens. Stephanie took her place alongside the other children, directing her sailboat in the lake with a long stick then running to the other side to retrieve her craft. My head was full of memories from years earlier when I sat around that lake with fellow students learning and laughing, sometimes until dark.

As the girls got older, they, too, became familiar with our friends at 8 à Huit as well as Madame Ankaoua and the Greek crepe man outside Luxembourg Gardens. Photos of my girls inside the crepe stand found their place in the photo album alongside those Heidi had taken of me years earlier in exactly the same spot. The girls learned a bit of traveler's French and started taking an interest in escargots as well as dishes cooked in white wine, cream, and butter.

FOREIGN STUDENTS - 1988

Amber Frangipane and Madame Ankaoua

In the spring of 1988, a letter arrived from Marie-Thérèse:

To our dear friend Barry:
*   Caroline and Danny would like to spend the month of August*
in the United States. Could they stay with you and your family?
*   Merci Beaucoup,*
*   Marie-Thérèse and Daniel*

Living in the suburbs of Tampa, Florida, where there's no viable public transportation system, we ended up providing a constant taxi service for the entire month of their stay. Danny was eighteen and Caroline sixteen, and

Daniel and Marie-Thérèse with Amber

neither of those two French-speaking full-blown teenagers
away from their parents for a month had any interest in
spending their days stuck in suburbia. They wanted Paris
without parents.

A day at Walt Disney World in Orlando did nothing to
impress the two of them. Danny laughed at the small Eiffel
Tower in EPCOT.

Caroline said, "It's all so fake. Where's the real Florida?"

Early one morning, we road-tripped north on US Highway 19 to see Devil's Millhopper, a true Florida sinkhole with an ecosystem more similar to North Carolina's due to its underground location. But their favorite part of the day was when we stopped at a gas station on the side of the highway. The station was open, but there was no attendant to be found.

"I'll be there in a minute," a man hollered from the creek alongside the station.

The three of us walked down to the creek, which fed into a large lake. Standing knee-deep in the water was a middle-aged man about six feet tall, three hundred pounds, wearing bib overalls and rubber boots. He was thrashing a dead chicken in the water and yelling, "Hector! C'mon, Hector!" in the general direction of the lake.

Seeing us there on the bank, he explained, "Hector is a twelve-foot gator. He comes every day to get his chicken. Hector! Hector!"

The thrashing paused when he left the lake to pump our gas.

"Must be on the other side of the lake right now."

He put the chicken down just long enough to fill up our tank. As we drove away, we could hear him once again yelling for Hector from the edge of the lake.

The gas-station incident only heightened the interest of the two city dwellers in seeing the real Florida, including real alligators. The next day found us in Myakka River State Park, renting a canoe large enough for me, Amber, Stephanie, Caroline, and Danny. With mating season in full swing, the river was full of alligators, some of which were fighting over their territory. Our foreign guests were intent on observing nature from the central location. At one point, our canoe was surrounded by gators, and Amber cried hysterically. Only then was I successful at convincing the Parisians to remain seated and paddle slowly toward the safety of the dock. I hoped that their next request might be something safer, like a butterfly farm or an orange grove.

One morning, about halfway through the month, I was having a peaceful breakfast poolside when Danny appeared.

"Where do you go?" Seeing the confused look on my face, he tried again. "Where do you go to hang out, to see friends?"

Danny's question caused me to look back on my time in Paris when I was twenty-one. There was Place de la Contrescarpe on Rue Mouffetard, always full of high school and college-aged kids in the six cafés lining the square. There was Place Saint-Michel and of course Luxembourg Gardens. In any of those places and many others, there was always the chance to find some friends or classmates. Our suburbs offered none of that, and we had no central meeting location for teenagers. I took them to the food court at the mall. It was the best I had to offer. For their remaining time in Florida, they were content to spend their days at the mall, although they rarely purchased anything.

On the way to Tampa Airport at the end of August, I asked them what they thought of Florida.

"I can't wait to get back to Le Mouffe and tell my friends about it!"

Danny's comment was all I needed to hear.

THE FRENCH BICENTENNIAL - JULY 1989

When the American Revolution began, France joined in to help fight the British. Their aid to the fledgling democracy was the equivalent of over one billion US dollars, leading to the decline of the French government's finances. A few years later, this debt played a significant role in the start of the French Revolution when, on July 14, 1789, the citizens of Paris stormed the Bastille. As thanks for General Lafayette's help fighting the British, Thomas Jefferson helped Lafayette draft the Declaration of the Rights of Man, the precursor to France's new constitution.

Recalling the American Bicentennial celebration in 1976, I thought it was only right that I should take my children to Paris to celebrate the French Bicentennial in 1989. A quick call to my friends Marie-Thérèse and Daniel from the 8 à Huit told me that all hotels in Paris had been booked for months.

"But Barry, Marie-Thérèse and I have an empty apartment right above the store. You and your family could just stay with us, if that's okay with you. We would love to see you again!"

Certainly the "Bicentenaire" would be something to photograph. But with the anticipated crowds—more than four hundred thousand were expected along the parade route—I knew my equipment might get stolen. A disguise was in order. I purchased a pink diaper bag and positioned a disposable diaper hanging out of an outside pocket and placed one of Amber's old stuffed bears in the other one. My camera and camcorder fit perfectly inside, and the disguise was complete. After all, who would want to steal a stinky diaper bag?

We arrived in Paris a few days before Bastille Day, referred to as Le Quatorze Juillet in France. Paris can be very hot in July, and that one was no exception. Like most apartments, ours had no air-conditioning, and we adjusted to the sounds of ambulances and police cars making an occasional run during the night.

When I awoke the next morning, I ran down the stairs and entered the boulangerie that used to supply Heidi and me with croissants every morning. The young girl who occasionally helped out was now running the bakery. We chatted for a few minutes while other customers waited, then I paid for my croissants and left. Instinctively, I walked the thirty feet or so to the entrance of Square Albin Cachot. A wave of emotions overcame me as I looked up at our old apartment. For a moment, I thought I saw Heidi waving out the window at me like she used to do when she would see me coming home. After regaining my composure, I turned away and went upstairs to deliver breakfast to my family.

July 13 started out just like any other Thursday in Paris with the notable exception of the millions of tourists from around the world who had come for the bicentennial cele-bration the next day. French President François Mitterrand hosted the inauguration of the new 2,700-seat Opera

Bastille with Placido Domingo among the performers. The new concrete-and-glass opera house was commissioned by Mitterrand to replace the smaller Opera Garnier commissioned by Napoleon III in 1860. The Garnier opera house with its golden foyer and baroque staircase now hosted dance events and ballet. It still had the underground lake made famous in Gaston Leroux's *Phantom of the Opera.*

By noon on July 13, the party was well underway. Streets were crowded, and many were open only to pedestrians. Aircraft old and new filled the skies for a continuous show over our heads. There appeared to be a genuine sense of community and pride among the French as they prepared for the historic day. Live music emanated from the bars and cafés on La Mouffe, with vendors selling spray cans of Silly String on every corner. Coincidentally, it was also my birthday, and the Latin Quarter was a perfect place to celebrate by dancing in the streets at Place de la Contrescarpe. Our two daughters completed the scene by covering the family and those around us with a thick layer of blue and red string foam. Long after midnight during the walk back to the apartment, I realized that the diaper bag containing my camcorder had been left at the edge of the fountain in front of La Contrescarpe. We rushed back to find it on the ground, covered with Silly String but with all the contents intact.

Bastille Day had finally arrived, waking us with the sounds of firecrackers from every direction. A parade greeted world leaders at La Défense, where a modern monument was inaugurated—La Grande Arche. The new arch was said to be "a monument to humanity and humanitarian ideals rather than military victories."

Taller than a football field is long, it was large enough that Notre Dame cathedral could fit inside. Now the "Historical Axis"—a straight line of monuments from the new Pyramid of the Louvre (completed just months earlier) through the Arc de Triomphe to La Grande Arche—was complete.

Still stinging from the French assistance to the United States during the American Revolution, British Prime Minister Margaret Thatcher took the opportunity during this grand French celebration to give a history lesson. She reminded the crowd that the British enshrined human rights in their Magna Carta in 1215 and added, "Let us not forget that the first revolution was that of 1688 and that it took place in England."

Oddly, her history lesson was not well received by the French press. But no matter. We had a parade to go to along the Champs-Élysées. The newspapers said the crowd was expected to grow to half a million people, so we started out early.

The automatic door of the Metro tried to close but bounced back after an encounter with a stepladder being carried by one of the passengers. In fact, a look around our subway car gave the impression that everyone was heading to a ladder convention instead of celebrating two hundred years of the rights of man.

Once on the Champs-Élysées, we were greeted by an ocean of people in every direction. The purpose of the ladders was now evident. Sage individuals who had carried them to the parade route were rewarded with an unobstructed view of the festivities. Others climbed the drainpipes loosely attached to the walls of the stores lining the street to get a better view. What could possibly go wrong when climbing twenty feet up a lead pipe likely installed hundreds of years ago on the side of building?

With no drainpipe and no ladder, it was as if we were not going to see the parade at all. Noticing our dilemma, a French couple offered to help. They had parked their Volkswagen van on a side street just off the parade route and let our two young daughters sit on the roof next to their own children to see the parade. Huge screens had been erected on the side streets, allowing the rest of us a view as well.

A float carrying a large red drum draped in black opened the parade, complete with hundreds of Chinese students, many of whom had been involved in the Tiananmen Square protests a few months prior. Later, a steam train sprayed snow onto the spectators, and 250 musicians from the Florida A&M band performed the moonwalk made famous by Michael Jackson. With more than six thousand participants and lasting over three hours, the parade ended with American opera singer Jessye Norman, draped in the blue, white, and red of the French flag, performing "La Marseillaise" at Place de la Concorde. At the other end of the Champs-Élysées, a dazzling display of fireworks over the Arc de Triomphe completed the show.

With the summer heat hovering around seventy-seven degrees, the intensely packed Metro on our return to the apartment was bearable except for the fireworks exploding continuously in our subway car. We decided to walk home, which was far cooler and less dangerous, and were treated to private fireworks displays throughout the skies of Paris for the entire journey. It was France's birthday, but Paris shared her gifts with us that night.

The morning paper confirmed that almost one million people had lined the streets for the festivities. Looking for something quieter to do on the day following the big party, the girls and I went to Musée Marmottan (which had become Musée Marmottan Monet) so they could see Claude Monet's *Impression, Sunrise* firsthand. I rushed to the ticket counter, excited to show my girls Monet's masterpiece. But when we entered the museum and went to see his work of art, all that hung on the wall was a sign indicating that the painting had been stolen in 1985, four years earlier. Stunned, I thought about how the painting had touched me when Heidi had brought me here in 1979. How could someone steal something so important to art, so important to the world, and keep it from public view?

"Dad, it's not coming back. Let's go," Stephanie said.

We returned to the apartment and packed for the long return trip to Florida the next day.

ÎLE SAINT-LOUIS - 1997

In the late nineties, I divorced and later remarried. With the children grown, I returned to Paris to show my new wife, Debbie, the city I had come to know and love. A small one-room flat on Île Saint-Louis would be perfect for our week in the City of Light. This forgotten and unloved island next to its little sister, Île de la Cité, is frequently ignored by tourists and Parisians alike. While Île de la Cité was graced with the impressive Notre Dame in the 1300s, Île Saint-Louis spent most of its lifetime hosting livestock and lumber. In fact, it was originally known as Île aux Vaches, or the island of cows. In the 1600s, Queen Marie de Médicis came up with a plan to turn the island into residences for the wealthiest of Parisians. After the French Revolution, the rich left, leaving it in the hands of artists, writers, and bohemians. More recent gentrification has raised prices and partially returned Île Saint-Louis to the rich.

Once we arrived at our front door directly on Rue Saint-Louis-en l'Île, it was apparent that our apartment was of the bohemian variety. The three-hundred-year-old stairway led to our loft, from which we could gaze at the pastries in the bakery on the floor below and smell the breads baking day and night. This resulted in us making quite a few visits downstairs. A mattress on the floor and a small table with two chairs completed the furnishings of our simple apartment.

We sampled the Tarte Normande, croissants au beurre, and baguettes from the bakery then continued with the cheeses from the local fromagerie. It was a bit of a mystery why that location in the center of Paris was barely an afterthought for most. A yellow tabby, the baker's cat, slept in the storefront window and exemplified the relaxed pace of the island.

"Deb, let's head to Bois de Boulogne. It's a great day for a picnic in the park. And while we're there, we can stop at the Monet family museum, Musée Marmottan Monet."

The park was a mix of thick woods and small lakes and even had an amusement park for children and adults alike. We settled near the waterfalls to enjoy our picnic before visiting the museum.

I explained to Debbie, "There are tons of great paintings to see here, but the one I really wanted you to see was stolen back in the 1980s. It's called *Impression, Sunrise*, and it gave its name to the Impressionist style of painting. The Impressionists such as Monet, Manet, and Renoir used quick brush strokes and focused on movement and the reflection of light. They painted their impressions of the subject, not a detailed rendition."

The guard, hearing our conversation, asked, "Are you looking for *Impression, Sunrise*? It was recovered in 1990 and has been hanging back on the wall of our museum where it belongs since 1991."

Sure enough, there she was, in her original location, albeit with a bit more protective rope than before. Staring at the recovered masterpiece, I briefly found everything once again right with the world. Taking my time, I studied her carefully, not knowing whether she would be stolen again before I made my next trip to the museum.

The sun had set behind Notre Dame by the time we returned to Île Saint-Louis. Debbie saw the sign for Bertillon and asked, "Is this the ice cream shop you always talk about? Let's each get a cone."

I got a wild strawberry cone, but for some reason, it didn't taste quite as sweet as the one Heidi bought me after her "no more English" declaration.

Immediately upon entering our apartment, Debbie encountered a visitor on our bed, one who had come in even with the door locked and the window shut. "Isn't that the baker's cat lying on our bed?"

"It sure is. He looks like he's sleeping. Maybe we shouldn't disturb him."

The cat, which I named Croissant, came and went frequently during the week. Admittedly, Croissant made our apartment feel a bit more like home.

I had read that some residents of the island had never left. A ninety-year-old woman who was interviewed said that she had ventured into Paris only twice in her life—once to get married and once years later for her husband's funeral. Because of the relaxed pace of the oasis in the heart of the city, I found it easy to understand her reasoning.

On one of our last nights in Paris, we hiked up to Montmartre to see the sunset from the top of the hill and to have a charcoal sketch of the two of us made in Place du Tertre. Evidently, we weren't the only ones with that idea. The crowd was so thick between Sacre Coeur and Place du Tertre that we were shoulder to shoulder with throngs of other tourists for almost an hour, missing the sunset entirely. But as the sky grew dark, the crowd dispersed, and several artists became available. We picked a scruffy old gentleman with a patch on his jacket and worn-out jeans to create our charcoal sketch. The man had a most interesting technique. He studied our faces for a few seconds then closed his eyes and drew, repeating the process until the sketch was complete. It was a fairly accurate sketch. I titled the work, *Impression, Eyes Shut.*

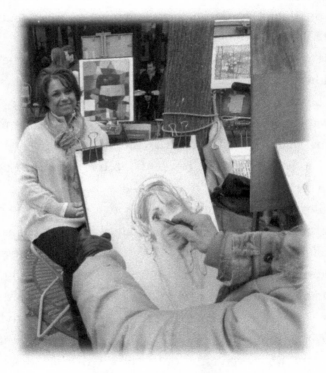

Debbie Frangipane, Place du Tertre

Although it had been roughly twenty years since my time at Alliance Française, I kept in touch with my old French teacher. Debbie and I had been invited by Madame Ankaoua and her husband, Maurice, for lunch in their place outside Paris. Maurice would cook, and Madame would have an opportunity to meet my wife.

On our last full day in Paris, Debbie returned from the morning market with a large bouquet of tulips. "Barry, look at the beautiful flowers I bought for your French teacher. But what's with the price of flowers? The signs all had prices a hundred times what I'm used to paying. Fortunately, the old man gave me a great deal on these tulips."

Chuckling, I recalled the explanation Heidi had given me decades ago after my first trip to the market and relayed to Debbie the story of francs anciens.

Promptly at noon, we arrived at the home of Madame Ankaoua and her husband, Maurice. A balding diminutive man, Maurice was the cook in the family. He greeted us at the door and held a tray of gougéres, small cheese-filled puff pastries, offering one to Debbie. As I handed the flowers to him, Maurice's smile accentuated his thin mustache as he looked over thick glasses to see Debbie enjoying his latest culinary creation.

Maurice and I went into the kitchen together. While I watched him prepare the main course, Madame Ankaoua gave Debbie a tour of their small third-floor home.

"Have you ever been to Versailles?" Madame asked Debbie over lunch.

"No, but I've heard it's absolutely gorgeous. Isn't there a long hallway full of glass mirrors made in Venice? I would love to see it!" Debbie replied.

"That settles it," Madame told her husband. "Maurice, let's take them to the Château of Versailles after dessert."

"But it's Monday, Loretta. Isn't Versailles closed today?"

"No matter, mon cheri. If it's closed, we can give Debbie and Barry a private tour."

"Oh, we appreciate the offer, Madame, but it isn't necessary. Barry and I will visit the château on another day, perhaps when it's open."

Madame Ankaoua wasn't listening. "Maurice, let's pack cheese, bread, grapes, and wine for the trip. Versailles is only twenty minutes from here."

With Versailles closed for the day, I wondered just what Madame had in mind for our private tour.

After gathering all the essential items, Maurice stepped into the driver's seat of their Renault 5 with Madame in the copilot's position. Throughout the long twenty-minute journey, she shouted instructions to her husband.

"Turn right, no, left! Left, Maurice, not right!"

"What's going on up there?" Debbie whispered. "Are they fighting?"

"Nope, Madame is just providing some navigational assistance."

"Here, stop here!" she commanded as the car veered right then came to a screeching halt in front of the locked entrance to the front of the château grounds. Suddenly, the chaos of the past twenty minutes of driving gave way to silence with the four of us staring at the lock on the gate.

"There must be a back entrance. Maurice, start the car."

In just a few sharp turns, we arrived well behind the château in a forested area with a dirt road marked "For use by firemen only in case of emergency."

"Turn here. This will lead to the château."

"But, but…"

Maurice was overruled.

The tiny Renault proceeded over the bed of leaves gently covering the surface of the dirt road and hiding the potholes underneath. Leaves flew around the car as we dodged the trees, with the Renault 5 bouncing left and right, throwing Debbie and me against the sides of the vehicle. We exited the other side of the forest and landed upon one of the walkways clearly designed for pedestrians.

"Are we supposed to be driving here?" Debbie asked me.

"Maurice, stop!"

A cloud of dust surrounded us. When the air cleared, a fountain appeared with gold statues of lizards shooting water into the air. Quickly, Debbie and I exited the car and ran to the edge of the fountain—partly due to its beauty and partly to distance ourselves from the illegal vehicle. Beyond the dust, the gardens descended gently, with more fountains extending out to the horizon.

"I would love to have something like this at our house," Debbie said.

Maurice laughed. "Over ten thousand workers were needed to build this palace and the surrounding gardens, and many of them died doing so. This is the Latona lizard fountain, carved from lead one hundred years before the revolution. It's said that Jupiter turned the inhabitants of Lycia into lizards for insulting Latona, his lover. More than two hundred sixty pumps were used just to get water to these artificial lakes. That's the château on top of the hill. From 1623 until 1789, France was ruled from here at Versailles, not Paris. The king was quite proud of Versailles. In fact, when he saw that his minister of finance built a château rivaling Versailles at Vaux-le-Vicomte, he imprisoned the minister until his death."

I was contemplating the dangers of insulting a Roman goddess, or of building a castle similar to Versailles, when, on Madame's command, we got back into the car.

"Go left, up there to Le Petit Trianon and Marie Antoinette's farmhouse."

Madame was still doling out directions while Maurice grew increasingly nervous, certain that the palace guards or the police would descend upon us at any moment. We reached the entrance to the queen's hamlet and stopped short in front of a small pedestrian walkway over a stream.

"Loretta, the sign says no bicycles. I really don't think that we should—"

"We're in a car, not a bicycle. Just cross the bridge!"

Parked directly in front of the Norman-style house built in 1783 as a playground for Marie Antoinette, we leaned against the car, eating the leftover pastries that Maurice had been kind enough to bring along. Looking up at the farmhouse windows, I imagined the guards alerting the queen.

"Madame, there is a strange horseless carriage in the courtyard with four people who clearly don't belong here. They seem to be eating some sort of cake."

"Oh, leave them alone. Let them eat cake."

"In the late 1700s, there were roughly four thousand people living in the royal court, a good part of them residing in the château. Marie Antoinette would come out here to the farmhouse when the stress of royal life was too much for her. She would dress as a shepherd and watch the cows being milked in the dairy outside her door," Maurice offered. "There's a man-made grotto near here with two separate entrances and a bed where the queen was suspected of having trysts with young men. In fact, she was in that grotto when she learned of the arrival of the revolutionary mob."

But on that day, there was no mob. Only the four of us and the ducks paddling slowly across the pond were enjoying the queen's idyllic, if artificial, farm village.

After retracing our bumpy route through the forest and back to the asphalt road, Madame helped her husband navigate us home. After bidding our friends au revoir, Debbie and I slowly walked to the Metro, allowing our stomachs to settle before boarding the train to Paris.

"Can we go see Versailles sometime?" Debbie asked.

"You mean just the two of us, when it's open?"

"Yes, when it's open."

The Frequent Guest

LETTERS TO MARCEL

Dear Marcel Marceau, I began my letter. *In 1979, I saw your movie* Scrooge, *where your alter ego Bip mimed all 17 parts. This work was a masterpiece. Is it possible to get a copy of the movie? I would like to share it with my two daughters.*

The letter was on its way to Marcel Marceau's manager, Sean Falkner, who had promised to deliver it to Marcel directly.

Less than a month had passed when a letter from France appeared in my mailbox.

My dear Barry,

How did you see the film? I'm so glad you enjoyed it. Sadly, the BBC has it tucked away in a drawer somewhere and won't let it out. It's just one of those things that we have to accept.

Yours Truly, Bip – Marcel Marceau

While excited to receive a letter from the most famous mime in the world, I knew he had worked hard on a masterpiece only to have it hidden away, which left me determined to get it out.

I contacted the BBC by phone, and they gave me an address to which I could write and request a copy.

We are sorry, but due to artists' rights, we cannot distribute copies of this work, the letter from the BBC read.

"Artists' rights?" I said aloud. "I'm staring at a letter from the only actor in the film, Marcel Marceau, who would like it to be made available."

But it was not to be. After I wrote additional letters and made more phone calls, it became evident that this work, once broadcast as an episode of the BBC's Omnibus educational program, would remain hidden. Over the following years, Marcel and I corresponded fairly frequently. When he performed in the United States, Sean always ensured that my wife and I had backstage passes. I in turn helped Sean in any way I could, supporting Marcel's foundation for keeping the art of mime alive.

There's an old saying, "Don't ever ask a mime to speak. Once he starts, he'll never stop." Marcel was no exception. His favorite topic was American politics. On rare occasions, he would tell us stories of his teenage years, smuggling more than seventy children over the border to Switzerland during WWII as part of the French Resistance. Solemnly, he described how he lost both of his parents at Auschwitz and changed his last name from Mangel to Marceau to hide his Jewish heritage and avoid being exterminated himself.

At his eightieth birthday party, held in Manhattan, Marcel looked around at the rich patrons of the arts who had come to meet the famous mime and be noticed themselves.

"Barry, I detest these parties. I don't even know any of these people. They want to talk but have nothing of import to say."

The smile on his face in front of the crowd belied this tired, aging star, torn between the fading limelight and his need for privacy. As my wife and I left the party, our friend Marcel, master of communicating without words, turned back to the crowd and tried to fit in.

THE IMPOSTER - 2000

"Barry, I need your help," said the voice on the phone. It was Sean Falkner. "More specifically, Marcel Marceau needs your help. Can you meet us in Paris in three weeks for an important meeting? Oh, and bring a suit. I'll explain everything when you get here."

It was a rainy spring day when Sean arrived at our hotel on Rue Cler, not far from the Eiffel Tower. He shuffled Debbie and me into a taxi, saying only, "We're heading to Marcel's house out in the countryside. His home is less than an hour from here. It'll all become clear after we arrive."

The old farmhouse was situated on about an acre of heavily wooded land in the town of Berchères. Marcel greeted us at the door then gave Debbie and me a tour of his home. Walking up the stairs in the vast two-story house, I was surrounded by photographs covering most every inch of the centuries-old stone walls. All the photos had something in common—Marcel. Over half a century of images showed him practicing his art everywhere from small stages to the big screen. I was still wondering why we were there when he called me aside and asked me to join him in his studio.

Marcel led me outside to a barn next to the main house. Entering the barn, I could see that he had transformed it into his workshop, with hardwood floors and ceiling-to-floor mirrors where he practiced his mime routines, and a hot tub for relaxing afterward. I followed him up the spiral staircase to the loft.

"This," said Marcel, "this is where I relax."

He moved aside the paintbrushes, paint, and empty canvasses to reveal dozens of watercolors, all painted by him upstairs in the barn.

"Look at this set of paintings, the seven deadly sins."

I found myself staring at seven dark paintings of *Pride*, *Greed*, *Lust*, *Envy*, *Gluttony*, *Wrath*, and *Sloth*. He then pulled out more-colorful free-flowing watercolors, which he titled *The Creation of the World*, *The End of the World*, *The Voyage of Bip*, and *The Circus Performers*. One of the paintings depicted Marcel on stage with hundreds of people in the audience, including Groucho Marx, Charlie Chaplin, and Buster Keaton in the front row! Pointing at the three, he confided, "These are my idols."

"Marcel," I said, astonished, "these are incredible! And

you have kept them hidden in your barn. We could form a traveling exhibition and give them the exposure they deserve."

He abruptly put them all away. "No. They do not leave my studio."

I wondered why he wanted to keep them hidden.

Marcel walked me back inside the house, where Debbie and Sean were waiting.

"Sorry to be so mysterious about the reason for asking you here," Sean told Debbie and me. "Let's sit down in the living room, and I'll explain."

After Marcel went into the kitchen to make coffee, Sean's expression turned serious, and his voice was hushed.

"A number of years ago, Marceau's Parisian manager tried to book him into a large venue in Paris. But Marceau's popularity, and that of mime in general in France, had waned, and the venues felt there was a strong chance of losing money on the event. Thus, no one was willing to take the risk to book him for a show. So, Marceau personally guaranteed the multiday event. Well, the show opened the day the Gulf War started, and everyone in Paris stayed home. This left him with a large debt to the venue, which he couldn't pay. Over the years, the debt increased, and he was taken to court and ordered to pay. If he cannot, the government will sell his possessions, including this home, to fulfill his obligations."

Debbie and I listened intently but still didn't understand my role. Sean certainly knew that I didn't have the money to help. And why was I asked to bring a suit?

Sean continued. "In order to avoid having the house repossessed, we need to show that we have in good faith been attempting to find alternative ways of obtaining the money. Tomorrow, the attorneys from a leading French merchandising firm will be here to try to negotiate a contract with Marceau. The attorneys speak only French, and I speak only English. Since you're bilingual, your role will be to listen to the offers and make a loud fuss if the offer is unfair to Marceau. Without your help, he's likely to agree to anything. You'll be introduced as his advisor from the United States. Rumor has it that they will be making him an unreasonable offer, and I'm counting on you to keep him out of worse trouble than he's already in. Can you do this for us?"

I looked at Debbie and whispered, "What do we have to lose?

"Let me make sure I understand, Sean. You want me to pretend that I'm an advisor from the United States and complain loudly about anything their attorneys offer that I consider unfair? And if we decline the offer, then what?"

"It's like this. Marcel is almost a public institution in France. Imagine the international press reaction if the French government repossessed the home of the most famous mime in the world. The court needs to show that they're trying to resolve the issue, but frankly, they would rather stall. Marceau is getting old, and the court would prefer to wait until after his death to repossess the home."

Marcel entered the room with espresso for everyone.

Sean winked at me, changing his request and asking,

"So, are you willing to listen to the attorneys tomorrow and translate for me what they have said?"

It was almost noon the following day when I arrived as planned at Marcel's second-floor office on the right bank in Paris. Sean was pleased to see me in my suit, dressed for the part that I was about to play. I was to be the advisor from New York, translating for Sean but mostly complaining about any wild proposals put forth.

In short order, the opposing attorneys arrived. After introductions and pleasantries, we all moved to a meeting room to start the talks. The two real attorneys sat on one side of the table, Sean and Marcel on the other. I chose to stand by the window overlooking the bustling streets below.

"Mr. Falkner," one attorney began, "we're big fans of Mr. Marceau. However, we understand that he's in a precarious financial position."

I turned from the window to show that I was listening intently.

The other attorney pulled out a pile of documents and explained, "Our client is famous for their high-end line of merchandise. Mr. Marceau is well-known and respected worldwide. The synergy between our client and Marceau will be profitable for all."

I translated all of this into English for Sean before asking the attorneys, "So, what is it exactly you are proposing?"

"We propose to completely pay off the debt, which is currently burdening Mr. Marceau, removing the imminent risk of him losing his house. He will be able to live peacefully, practicing his art without this financial concern."

Marcel looked interested.

"And in return?" I asked.

"And in return, your respected client would agree to act in commercials designed and produced by our client to promote our products. Of course, any live or recorded shows in which he wishes to perform would have to be approved by our client to avoid any potential conflict of interest."

I paced the floor, stopping for a moment to gaze out the window for dramatic effect. Internally, I wondered what the heck I had gotten myself into.

"Am I to understand that you want full artistic control of the master's work while relegating him to being a clown in an unlimited number of your commercials solely to support your client's products? And that you could choose to deny him any work outside of that that he performs for your commercials?" I paused for effect. "No! This is not the way to treat an artist of his caliber! This man is a legend, and he should not be constrained in this manner. Absolutely not!" I winked at Sean.

Lawyer number two gathered up the documents and put them back in his briefcase. "We understand your position. Au revoir, messieurs."

With terse handshakes, the two attorneys left the building.

"Nice work!" Sean shook my hand before I explained everything to Marcel.

Debbie, Marcel Marceau, Barry at Berchères

That night, Marcel, Sean, Debbie, and I celebrated over dinner at Marcel's favorite Moroccan restaurant, laughing about the outcome of my Parisian acting debut.

"Marcel, would you mind taking a picture of Debbie and me with my camera?"

He was ready to take the photo when Debbie asked him to sit next to us so that Sean could take a shot of all three of us together.

"Marcel," I asked, "how many people have had their photo taken with you? Tens of thousands?"

"At least," he replied modestly.

"But how many people have pictures of themselves taken by you?"

"Probably none."

I continued, "Exactly. Debbie, Marcel is a mime. It only makes sense that he would take the picture and not be in it.

What a collector's item we'll have—a photo taken by Marcel Marceau!"

Debbie rolled her eyes. "That's the dumbest idea you've had all day."

My opportunity passed, but we do have a boring photograph of the three of us together at dinner.

Marcel Marceau lived out the rest of his life in the four-hundred-year-old farmhouse and was never bothered by the government again.

HOT AIR

All that hot air emanating from the attorneys had given me an idea. Debbie and I would take a balloon ride in the Loire Valley. Château d'Artigny was the perfect place to begin. Roughly an hour south of Paris outside of Tours and built in the eighteenth century, the castle was the home of François Coty, the perfume magnate. Situated on top of a hill overlooking meticulously manicured gardens, it had become a hotel in 1960. We would drive to the château, take a leisurely stroll in the gardens, and finish the evening by dining at the on-premise restaurant. The dawn would find us boarding a hot air balloon on the grounds of the majestic Château de Chenonceau. At least, that was the plan.

Upon entering the rotunda of Château d'Artigny, I looked up to see a dome in *tromp l'oeil* featuring a painted balcony complete with frescoes of the Coty family and friends looking down at us peasants below. Our room offered a beautiful view of the gardens and the valley, although the fog settled in as the evening arrived, making it difficult to see much of anything outside. I could easily have imagined Napoleon staying in our room, except of course that he died before it became a hotel.

The next morning, we were enjoying coffee and pastries, looking forward to our day's adventure, when our server approached the table.

"Monsieur Frangipane, I am sorry to disrupt your breakfast, but we have a message for you from the ballooning company."

The message knocked the wind out of our sails, at least for the time being.

"We are sorry for the inconvenience, but due to fog, the balloon trip has been rescheduled. The new meeting point will be in front of the Moret-Sur-Loing train station at 9 a.m. tomorrow."

With our stay at Château d'Artigny over, we drove back to our Paris hotel with a plan to take the train to Moret-Sur-Loing in the morning.

The driver picked up us and four other guests in front of the train station as planned at 9 a.m. "There's been a slight change of plans. Due to the wind direction, we can't take off from the grounds of Château Chenonceau. But don't worry. We've found an alternate launch point."

As we drove through the valley for over an hour, I wondered from which picturesque castle we would be launching. Would it be Azay-Le-Rideau, the glorious château built on an island in the Indre river, or maybe the

Château de Chaumont that I remembered from the EPCOT movie about France? No, I was certain we would depart from the grounds of Château de Chambord, which rivaled Versailles in both size and beauty.

We exited the van in a swampy area next to a ditch at the edge of a farm. There were no castles in sight, only mosquitoes, which kept us busy during the long wait for the balloon to arrive by truck and be prepared for launch. Once the mosquitoes were sufficiently fed, the balloon with its six passengers and pilot rose from the mud and into the sky.

Floating over the length of the Loire Valley, we were treated to views of castles in every direction. At times, the pilot raised us high above the ground, allowing us to see for miles. Other times, he dropped down low enough for us to hear the farmers shout "Bonjour!" as we drifted past. As sunset approached, the balloon cast a long shadow over the sunflower fields. Admittedly, I was getting nervous about missing our train as children in pajamas on their bicycles chased our balloon and watched us descend. After floating at less than one meter above the sunflowers, we landed along a dirt road.

The basket tipped over, quickly dispensing all of us passengers onto the ground. After cleaning the newly acquired dirt off of each other, we enjoyed a celebratory glass of champagne with the local farmers before the driver dropped off Debbie and me back at the Moret-sur-Loing train station.

"The last train to Paris will be coming soon, so don't miss it!" she yelled out the window before driving off.

The ticket counter was closed, and we were the only ones waiting alongside the tracks. Night descended, and after an hour or so, a man with a cane hobbled past us and said, "No more trains."

"Pardon?" I asked.

"There are no more trains tonight. You've missed the last train."

Hungry and exhausted, we walked into town to plan our next move, asking a bartender for advice.

"You won't be able to get to Paris tonight. Stay at a hotel and take the train in the morning. There's a motel about two kilometers down the road called F1. I'll call and ask them to save a room for you."

We walked a bit more than a mile in the dark, realizing that the night's lodging might not match the luxury of our previous night at Château d'Artigny.

"F1" was short for Formula One. Our room was equipped with two bunk beds made to look like race cars. A small television hung in the corner, and a small sink completed the furnishings. The walls were made of molded plastic, while the shower and toilet were down the hall.

Since we hadn't expected to spend a night outside of Paris, we had no changes of clothes, and Debbie had no contact lens solution. I improvised by putting water in two plastic cups I found in the lobby. Debbie put one lens in each cup before climbing the ladder to the upper race car for a well-deserved rest.

The next morning, our breakfast in the lobby consisted of a counter with a loaf of white sandwich bread and a jar of strawberry jam. A pot of American-style coffee appeared to be the only beverage. We skipped breakfast and walked to the station, Debbie carefully carrying her only luggage— two plastic cups containing her contact lenses. Finally on board a train to Paris, Debbie and I chuckled while recalling the highs and lows of our balloon trip in the Loire Valley.

THE LAST PEEPEE IN PARIS - 2005

"Je pisse, donc je suis" (I pee, therefore I am)
—Sign outside the public restrooms in Nice, France

————————◆————————

Working as a computer project manager for a new company in Florida, I traveled three or four times each year to our subsidiary in Wales. This gave me the opportunity for frequent stopovers in Paris. Having trained as a chef at the Culinary Institute of America, Debbie was working in the kitchens of Walt Disney World in Florida and had an extremely busy schedule. When her work permitted, she joined me. One such trip was in 2005.

The pissoirs used by Parisian men to relieve themselves for more than 150 years have all but disappeared. In fact, the dark-green double pissoir outside La Prison de la Santé on Boulevard Arago is the only one left. Killed off by the feminist movement, they've been replaced by a few hundred toilet stalls scattered throughout the city. With the cost of using them at one euro per pee, many men have gone back to the age-old Parisian tradition of peeing in the streets. Women, however, can use the new coin-operated toilets, assuming one happens to be nearby and assuming one has a one-euro coin.

"I have to pee," Debbie announced as we walked the streets on the warm summer morning.

I found her one of those new coin-operated toilets, but the line was long and wasn't moving. We had heard that sometimes, the homeless used them for shelter and stayed in them all night.

"This isn't going to work. Let's go to a café, and you order a coffee while I use the restroom."

Dutifully, I drank an espresso while Debbie used the WC. As the day got warmer, Deb made sure to drink many bottles of water to stay hydrated.

"There's another one of those toilets—with no line," she said.

I handed her one euro.

After depositing the coin and opening the door, she took a whiff and exited immediately. "It's disgustingly filthy. Let's find another café."

That routine continued every hour, with me drinking shot after shot of espresso while Deb used the facilities in different corners of the city.

My heart was racing and my hands were shaking when, in the late afternoon, my wife requested that I order yet another coffee at a nearby café.

"No!" I yelled. "I can't have another coffee!"

She quickly observed that I was well overcaffeinated and ordered me a decaf coffee before entering the restroom. For the rest of the night, I switched to lemon soda for our hourly pit stops.

In 2006, Paris initiated many changes in their quest to improve the urinary experiences of the Parisians of both sexes. The outdoor toilets no longer required a coin to enter, and the doors opened automatically after fifteen minutes to help prevent their use as a hotel. Some were even equipped with background music.

With all the fuss over nearly two centuries of men-centric piss points in Paris, in 2018, they returned but in a modified form. Paris installed at least five flower boxes with absolutely no privacy and a urinal-style opening on the side. With this new invention, men could pee and water the flowers at the same time. The Paris City website stated that "each year, the pee from one person provides enough nutrients to fertilize 400 square meters of wheat."

Debbie still prefers the espresso-WC team sport. I, on the other hand, have started taking medication to stabilize my heartbeat.

SPRING IN PARIS - 2013

Morning snow flurries drifted past the window of our third-floor apartment on Rue de la Montagne Sainte Geneviève, making their way slowly to an untimely death on the pavement below. Sipping our coffees beside a tiny heater in the kitchen, Debbie and I mapped out our week of culinary research. My wife had taken over a restaurant in central Florida and was looking for inspiration from Parisian chefs old and new. The plan was to visit ten restaurants in five days with a bit of sightseeing in our spare time.

We dove right in, starting at Le Comptoir du Relais Saint Germain, near Odeon. The escargot in parsley butter arrived first. When the aroma hit me, I instantly drifted back to the day that Thierry Lepage of Dosapro served me escargot for the first time back in 1979. I hardly noticed when the hard-boiled eggs with fried onions were delivered. The food journey continued with tender braised lamb and dried fruits followed by roast veal perfectly paired with mushrooms and nuts. By the time we finished our balsamic-vinegar-infused panna cotta and coffee-flavored crème brûlée, the afternoon was heading into evening. Soon, we would need to work our way to Spring Paris, Chef Daniel Rose's hideaway near the Louvre.

Still full from lunch when we arrived for our eight o'clock reservations made months in advance, we were presented with a tasting menu including hake with cucumber, and mullet with peppered artichokes. The grilled mullet melted in my mouth, leaving the flavor of the artichokes to kick in immediately afterward. For me, that was the star of the show. Main courses continued with lamb with Greek yogurt and kalamata olives, and milk-fed veal topped with chanterelles. The most memorable of the four desserts was the strawberry-basil sorbet. The sweetness of the berries was a perfect match for the savory flavor of the fresh basil. Chef Rose had created an open kitchen and constantly experimented with new combinations of flavors, textures, and colors. Notwithstanding any dietary restrictions, every diner was presented with some of the most masterfully created items ever to come out of a modern French kitchen.

Taking a taxi back to the apartment, we realized that performing in-depth research at two restaurants every day would be a pace impossible to sustain. The next morning, while at a picnic table outside an artisan pastry shop and eating our swirled pastries flavored with lemon, raspberry, chocolate pistachio, and the standard pain au rhum raisin, we painfully slashed our list of restaurants in order to reduce our research and hopefully our waistlines as well.

We took the afternoon off, climbing the grand staircase at the Garnier opera house to see the colorful ceiling frescoes created by Marc Chagall in 1963. Chagall emigrated to Paris in 1923 to escape the anti-Semitism in his home country of Belarus. His colorfully fluid ceiling panels paid tribute to fourteen master composers including Bizet, Verdi, Mozart, Ravel, and Debussy. Chagall was quite passionate about his contribution to the Opéra Garnier and said, "Now I offer this work with gratitude to France and the École de Paris, without which there would have been neither color nor freedom for me." In the center of the fresco hung the fifteen-thousand-pound chandelier Heidi had pointed out to me roughly thirty-five years earlier. I thought about the night we watched *La Bohème* in 1979 while standing in the balcony and wondered silently where my old roommate might be and if she even remembered me.

After we enjoyed a light lunch at the newly opened L'Opéra Restaurant, dinner found Debbie and me back at work at the renowned Chez Georges on Rue Le Mail. Chez Georges has been cooking classic French dishes for roughly fifty years. It was a perfect place to research poached eggs in wine sauce, duck breast with mushrooms cooked in duck fat, and beef filet in a mustard cream cognac sauce. The quality of the ingredients and the years of experience of the staff produced delicate flavors that we couldn't get enough of. Nobody cooks duck like the chefs of Paris. Nobody. Our studies completed with baba au rum cakes for Debbie and profiteroles oozing a warm dark chocolate sauce for me.

The following morning as I enjoyed my croissant and coffee, I recalled memories of the riots of 1979 while looking at the street below. Five or ten people were protesting nuclear energy, carrying signs, blowing whistles, and yelling something unintelligible through a bullhorn. But no matter, we had reservations at L'Ami Jean, home to Spanish-born chef Stephane Jego.

In the waning days of that week, we only managed to get to L'Ami Jean, Le Bal Café, Neva Cuisine, and Cèpe Et Figue. We were in such a food coma on our day of departure that while taking our luggage to the street, I managed to lock us out of the apartment, with my wallet, the keys, and our passports still inside. After a two-hour wait for the apartment owner to arrive with a spare set of keys, we somehow made it to the airport in time to catch our flight back to Florida.

Looking out the window at the French countryside well below us, I asked Debbie if she felt inspired by her trip and if she would be putting any of those inspirations on her menu.

"I'm still so full that I don't ever want to see food again!"

We didn't discuss food or much of anything else for the remainder of the flight. Looking at the four remaining pastries that I had brought on board, I thought about how my life had changed from the days when I was begging for food in Paris with my Popeye puppet. Sometimes, when we look back, we realize that our hardest times might have been the best of times.

Debbie's own version of lamb with Greek yogurt and

olives did make it onto the menu in her Florida restaurant, as did her duck breast paired with duck confit ravioli in a Gorgonzola cream sauce topped with duck cracklings.

DINNER WITH FRIENDS - 2014

We all need a place that, when we're there, envelops us like a lover's embrace. A place where there's no need to rush, no need to visit monuments or tourist attractions. A place to relax with friends or where it's sufficient to close our eyes, smile, and say, "I'm home."

It had been a long, hard business trip in Wales, after which I was looking for just that sort of relaxation in Paris. Being on my own in Paris, I had no way of enjoying Debbie's lamb dish or the duck confit ravioli in Gorgonzola. However, a new company called Vizeat had been created by Camille Rumani and Jean-Michel Petit and offered to pair visitors with Parisian families who would, for a price, invite them to dinner in the host family's home. It reminded me of my experience with the "Spend a Weekend with a French Family" program back in 1979. So I signed up to have dinner with a French couple in an upscale part of Paris, just a few hundred yards from Musée Marmottan Monet, at the edge of Bois de Boulogne. I would be sure to arrive with bread and flowers.

The fog hid the landscape as I traveled toward Paris on the Metro from Aéroport Charles de Gaulle. As I walked from the Metro to the hostel that would be my home for the next week, a cold wind blew the rain onto my face. The hostel was conveniently located near Place d'Italie, with rooms containing two or four beds and a bathroom/shower inside the room, and croissants with coffee and juice were served in the morning. The hostel was a place where I wasn't alone, a place where I could meet fellow travelers from around the world.

After settling in, I made a trip across town to Du Pain et Des Idées, an artisan patisserie-boulangerie near Place de la République. They still made perfectly crafted breads using age-old recipes long since abandoned by many chain boulangers who now sold par-baked products premade and then frozen at a central location to be rewarmed before sale to unsuspecting customers. The baguettes at Du Pain et Des Idées were nice and crunchy on the outside while soft and chewy on the inside.

I picked up two for my dinner appointment as well as a chocolate-pistachio pastry and a butter croissant for a snack. The rain departed and a rainbow arrived as I sat along the banks of the Canal Saint Martin to relax and enjoy my croissant. A bouquet of tulips from the street market at Place d'Italie completed my purchases for the night's encounter.

Back at the hostel, I reviewed the email from Marie-Claude with the night's invitation.

"We'll see you between 8:00 and 8:30. We looked at your profile and saw that you have written a book on Venice. We're absolutely fond of Italy and want to hear all about your book."

Their street was meticulously curated and lined with weeping purple beech trees. The gardens and pavement were so clean that it looked more like a street in Copenhagen than one in Paris. I rang the doorbell promptly at eight o'clock and handed my hosts the flowers and baguettes acquired that morning. The apartment was furnished with the finest in crystal and blown glass chandeliers as well as china cabinets and end tables like the ones I had seen in the fancy stores on the right bank, where I knew better than to even enter. Marie-Claude and her husband, Pierre, appeared to be in their early sixties and spoke French along with some Italian and English. They had also invited to dinner four of their friends who had apartments in Venice and were leaving in a few days for Italy. The six of them dressed and spoke like those in the upper part of French society but appeared at ease dining with a more bohemian author like me. Over the next four hours, we enjoyed each other's company and discussed the differences between the butter-and-cream-based cuisine of northern France and the olive-oil-based cuisine of Italy. One of the couples favored the richness of the Normandy creams, while the other touted the deep flavor and health benefits of a high-quality Italian olive oil made from taggiasca olives.

We started new friendships and ate course after course of home-cooked classic French dishes. The first was cassoulet au poulet, a hearty stew made with chicken, sausages, beans, and duck fat. The pommes dauphines, or fried potato puffs, were light and fluffy, balancing the richness of the stew. Taking a break from eating for a few minutes, we all enjoyed a shot of Calvados, which burned a hole through our main course, preparing us for dessert. One of the couples asked about my book on Venice. Finally, we finished our discussions when Marie-Claude brought out the tarte tatin, a classic French version of a caramel apple pie. Before I caught the last train back to the hostel, we hugged and promised to see each other again. Relaxing in bed, I reflected on an evening of dinner and wine with new friends. I was home.

The next morning in the hostel restaurant, I enjoyed a breakfast of two butter croissants, French bread with butter and jam, juice, two cups of coffee, and a bit of cereal. True, most of the travelers never looked up from their cell phones, even though we were seated at a communal table. It felt odd to be surrounded by so many people but with hardly anyone interested in having a face-to-face conversation, quite different from my meal the previous night. I left Place d'Italie and walked through the street market on Boulevard Auguste Blanqui. The aroma of hot roasted chicken, aged cheeses, and grilled sausages continue to make it my favorite street market. Hours later, I ended up near the gates of Luxembourg Gardens, where a crowd of travelers with suitcases outside the Metro station attempted to hail taxis to the airport.

"Qu'est-ce qui ce passe?" I asked a man with two suitcases and a young daughter in tow.

"There was a suspicious package found on the RER B Metro line to the airport, so it's shut down. We need to find a taxi to the airport. But all the taxis have disappeared."

With no taxis and no functioning train to the airport, the crowd was certain to miss their flights. I wished them well but continued my personal journey to the crepe stand.

"Et ton oncle, ça va?" I asked my friend at the stand about his uncle, my crepe maker for thirty-five years.

"He's traveling around England. Since he retired, he never stays still for long. I'll tell him you said hello next time he returns to Paris. How about a butter-sugar crepe today?"

I had finished the crepe by the time I arrived at the café inside the gardens. Enjoying a hot chocolate, I read the day's *Le Parisien* newspaper.

"Taxis impose slowdown and manifestation today in Paris," claimed the headline.

To protest the French government's decision on the previous Friday not to punish Uber, a new phone-app-based ride service that used private drivers and paid no taxes, the Parisian taxis had instituted a slowdown of service. I wondered if the suspicious package on the Metro and the taxi strike were somehow related. On a typical day, the RER B Metro line transported just under one million travelers. Shutting down both taxi and train service would effectively close access to the airport. That evening, I discussed the situation with the hostel receptionist. My international flight was to leave the following morning.

"But why take the Metro to the airport? I can get you a shuttle that will pick you up right here at the front door of the hostel. It's much easier, trust me. Your flight leaves at ten fifteen tomorrow morning. I'll have him pick you up at seven thirty so you'll have plenty of time for coffee and a croissant at the airport."

Admittedly, the receptionist's idea was attractive due to the "suspicious package" found on the Metro earlier that day, even if the shuttle was three times the price of the Metro.

To be certain that the shuttle driver didn't leave without me, I was out in front of the hostel at 7:20 a.m., watching snow flurries melt as they hit the sidewalk. At 7:30, there was no sign of the shuttle. At 7:40, the hostel receptionist placed a call.

"Monsieur, there was a bit of traffic, but the shuttle will be here in ten minutes. "

At 8 a.m., he placed another call. "He's three minutes away."

"Will he be going straight to the airport, or does he have other stops? Maybe I should take a taxi." It amazed me that in a city as big as Paris, there was no foolproof way of getting to the airport.

"Yes, nonstop to the airport after he picks you up."

I placed my bags in the shuttle at 8:15. He then drove into the center of the town instead of getting on the bypass road.

"J'arrive... cinq minutes, madame."

I heard him on the phone, promising another passenger that he would arrive in five minutes, even though traffic in front of Notre Dame was at a complete standstill. Fifteen minutes later, after loading up the additional passengers somewhere near Chatelet, he offered, "Don't worry. You will still have time for a café at the airport. You will think of me while you are having your café, monsieur?"

I looked up to respond while the Uber app was downloading to my phone.

"Oh yes, I will most certainly be thinking of you. That's for sure."

I arrived at the airport at 9:45, rushed through passport control and security, and was the last person to board my flight. Sitting in my center seat on the plane at 10:30, having had no time for a café or a croissant, I decided the shuttle driver was right. I was thinking of him.

OH CHRISTMAS TREE - DECEMBER 23, 2014

Debbie and I went to Paris to stay for Christmas and New Year's Eve at a rental apartment on Rue Galande, in the fifth arrondissement near Notre Dame. We arrived on separate flights—me from Wales and Debbie from Florida—and met up at Charles de Gaulle airport. After taking the train into the city, we surfaced at Metro station Cité, in the center of the Marché aux Fleurs. There weren't many flowers at the market, but there were quite a few Christmas trees.

"Let's get a Christmas tree. It'll be fun to decorate a tree in Paris!" Debbie suggested, dragging her luggage out of the way of the other market shoppers.

"But the apartment's only three hundred square feet. Where will we put a tree? And besides, it's on the fifth floor, and there's no elevator. We are not getting a tree!"

We returned to the marché on Christmas Eve. The lady at the flower market had roughly seven trees to choose from. Debbie picked out one, and it would be hoisted up to the fifth floor and live out the remainder of its short life at our apartment. I thought about how we were going to transport it.

Fortunately, Parisians don't use the "tree, bucket, and dirt" system for holding up the tree as they do in some countries. Rather, they simply drill a hole in a block of wood and place the tree in the hole.

"So, what happens now?" I asked the man who wrapped the tree with gauze in preparation for its final journey.

He stepped back from the tree and raised his hands in the air.

"It's out of my hands at this point. Your wife sure did pick out a big tree, n'est-ce pas?"

The tree was only a bit taller than me, although quite a bit wider. Debbie grabbed the top while I grabbed the trunk, and we trudged back with the newest member of our family in hand.

Our route, however, took us directly in front of Notre Dame, where throngs of tourists admired the tree Vladimir Putin had donated to Paris Christians in the name of Russia. Notre Dame could not afford the eighty thousand euro for a Christmas tree and had made a request to the public for donations. The French speculated that after the bad press Russia had received for their invasion of Ukraine earlier in the year, Putin felt that his gesture might provide a bit of goodwill between the two countries. I felt certain Debbie would do a better job decorating our tree than had those who decorated the sad-looking tree from the Russians.

"Oh Christmas tree, Oh Christmas tree, how heavy are thy branches," I sang as we carried the tree across the square. The lyrics weren't perfect, but they did help me keep my mind off the sharp pain in my lower back.

Leaving the tourists, Notre Dame, and Putin's tree behind, Debbie and I stopped at the base of the stairs leading up to our apartment.

"Do you think we could just decorate it right here in the public stairwell?" she asked, catching her breath.

"Well, Deb, it's not a bad idea. That way, everyone could enjoy it."

Somehow, we managed to make it up the seventy-five winding steps to our humble abode without dropping the tree—or falling on our faces.

The stores in Paris were packed with shoppers on Christmas Eve as we searched for decorations and lights. On previous trips, the stores would have been filled with French, Germans, and Brits. But that year, the economy was tight, and it appeared that most of the people carrying bags were from Asia, primarily China. The Germans were missing entirely, and the Brits and Americans didn't appear to be purchasing very much. Clearly, for the young Chinese, it was their first experience in Paris. Bubbling with laughter, shopping bags in hand, they ran from corner to corner, taking pictures of every monument from every possible angle. A new generation from a different part of the globe was enjoying the City of Light.

The sidewalks of the Champs-Élysées were so full that it was difficult to move in any direction at the Christmas market. While admiring the gold twinkling lights in the hundreds of trees lining the boulevard, I felt something stiff pressing against the back of my jacket. I turned to see if someone was trying to steal my wallet, and the barrel of a machine gun was pointed at my derrière. Thankfully, it was in the hands of a policeman, one of two who just happened to be behind me, trying to work their way through the crowd. We left the market in search of a neighborhood with fewer crowds and fewer machine guns.

After multiple trips to BHV, Tati, and other department stores, we accumulated three strings of lights, a few strands of white feathers, and black ornaments with silver glitter. Tree-topping angels evidently did not exist in France (even the trees in the store windows were topless), so we decorated a small white wreath with battery-operated lights, and voila, our first Christmas tree in Paris!

"Oh, by the way, I invited two nice guys I met on the plane to our apartment for Christmas dinner. You know, no one should be alone for Christmas," Debbie mentioned casually.

"But if there are two of them, how can they be alone?" I uttered to no one in particular. In reality, I was used to Debbie inviting strangers to dine with us.

Debbie was busy planning the next day's dinner menu.

"We'll have oysters with a sauce of shallots cooked in

cider, Calvados, and crème fraîche garnished with rosemary white chocolate pearls, followed by roast duck stuffed with peaches and topped with a currant-and-wine-reduction sauce. Then we'll finish off the dinner with a cheese-and-salami tray, crostini with leeks, and an endive salad with walnuts and Comté. Oh, let's remember to get a Bûche de Noël at the boulangerie for dessert."

There's something about having guests over to your apartment for the first time that makes it feel like home, and that was how it felt for Deb and me.

I got up early on Christmas Day for a coffee at Café Panis, directly across the river from Notre Dame. Paris sang to me that day. As the bells of the cathedral rang out, I sipped my café au lait in full view of the French symbol of Christianity. Through countless revolutions and wars, through a series of miracles, she still stood. People arrived in a steady stream from every direction to stand in the square and admire her. But on that day, they were doing more than taking the obligatory snapshot before boarding a bus and heading to another monument. They were drawn by some invisible connection to her past, to her reason for existence. The bells echoed through the surrounding streets as if to tell everyone, "Wake up! Come join us in celebration."

Most of the local food stores in Paris were open Christmas morning—bakeries, seafood stores, butchers, cheese vendors, actively selling their goods until early afternoon. That was not because vendors were chasing that extra euro but rather because Parisians insist on fresh bread, meats, and seafood for their holiday meals. So, just like the locals, I went in search of the best oysters, duck, and baguettes in our part of town and found them all at Place Maubert. The man at the poissonnerie had high-quality oysters from Normandy.

"Since today is Christmas, I'll open them all for you, no charge. Go have a coffee at the café and come back. Better still, have two coffees, and your oysters will be ready."

La Maison d'Isabelle provided two baguettes cooked to perfection, while another patisserie around the corner sold the traditional Christmas logs (cakes called Bûche de Noël) made primarily of chocolate, flour, chocolate shavings, butter, cocoa, heavy cream, and more chocolate. The line went out the door and around the corner. When I arrived inside, it was evident that the storefront was rented solely as a place for customers to pick up their logs on Christmas Day. Nothing other than Bûche de Noël wrapped in decorative foil was available, and workers rushed to get everyone their products as quickly as possible. When I finally returned to the poissonnerie for my oysters, they were wrapped and ready, and the store was preparing to close.

Our new friends Peter and Joe arrived at our apartment as planned at three o'clock, and the food continued to come out of our tiny kitchen for hours. A look out the window over the rooftops of Paris showed that the clouds had taken Christmas night off, allowing the quarter moon to display itself brightly overhead.

Joe explained that he was an editor at National Public Radio, while Peter was a ballet dancer and art teacher originally from Mexico. Peter and Debbie shared their thoughts on interior decorating, and Joe and I discussed Paris. Joe marveled at the exquisite presentation of oysters with white chocolate pearls, while my favorite was the simple duck-and-peach combination with wine reduction. No one seemed too interested in the store-bought Bûche de Noël. The four of us finished the evening by strolling past Notre Dame and the ice rink in front of Hotel de Ville. Joe and Peter continued to their hotel at Les Halles, leaving Debbie and me to walk under the starlit skies. Standing at the edge of the Seine with the moon shining between the two towers of the cathedral, Debbie kissed me and said,

"This has been a wonderful Christmas. We've made new friends in Paris. If I could just learn the language, I could live here."

SHAKESPEARE AND COMPANY

Earlier in 2014, I had decided to write this book. I found that writing in Paris was certainly easier than attempting to be creative at a chain coffee shop back in Florida. When I was sitting at Les Deux Magots on Boulevard Saint-Germain, staring out at the Saint-Germain-Des-Prés church celebrating its 1,000th birthday, inspiration came easy. The rich were inside the café, the poor outside, and the latest fashions sashayed by. It was easy to understand why Les Deux Magots was a great place for Hemingway, Sartre, and others to write. But when the café was too crowded, I wrote at the bookstore Shakespeare and Company, which Heidi had pointed out to me in 1979.

The bookstore is still staffed by an eclectic and passionate group. Before their shifts and during breaks, they can be seen curled up in a corner chair with a cup of tea, reading Goethe, Miller, or Dostoevsky. While the current version of the bookstore was opened in 1951, it carries on the tradition of the original Shakespeare and Company, run by Sylvia Beach from 1919 until 1940, when it closed due to the German occupation of France. It is now run by Sylvia Beach Whitman, whose father opened the current store and named his daughter after the original owner.

When I discovered an old writing desk and typewriter upstairs by the window in the Sylvia Beach Memorial Library, I knew I had found a magical place. And after receiving permission from the staff, I worked into the night writing there, surrounded by great works of authors from years gone by. The room was lined with wall-to-wall bookshelves with built-in benches at the base. As I looked out the window at Notre Dame and the surrounding buildings giving a golden glow, words flew out of the pen and onto the page. I could almost hear Ernest speaking with Sylvia about his latest book and promising to pay her for the books he had borrowed but didn't return. Not only did Sylvia allow writers such as Gertrude Stein and F. Scott Fitzgerald to borrow books, but she also allowed them to

The Frequent Guest

sleep in between the shelves at night when times got tough, a tradition that continues today.

While I was writing, a visitor would occasionally stop by, find a book, and read in one of the few comfortable chairs or benches. A small gray cat ate and drank from the bowls under my desk and made himself at home for a few minutes in the cushioned chair next to me. When he jumped down, a strong odor filled the air, and there was a large puddle on the seat cushion. I made a sign from a small piece of paper reading simply "No" and carefully placed it at the edge of the chair so that no one would have their experience dampened by the gray cat's urinary activities.

After a half hour or so, an employee came by and replaced both the cushion and the cat. The new cat, a large white one, immediately jumped onto my lap and went to sleep as I wrote. I have continued to write at that location for almost ten years, whenever I am in Paris.

Déjà Vu

NEW YEAR'S EVE

With my writing done for the day, I joined Debbie and our friend Pauline in a restaurant on the edge of Place de L'Ecole Militaire. Born in the south of France, Pauline was in her twenties and had never been to Paris. We had invited her to spend a few days with us at the end of the year. She asked the waiter what he recommended for dinner.

He replied, "Nothing, really. It's my first week working here, and I don't care much for the food."

In the end, his assessment of the quality was fairly accurate. After our meal, we rushed to find a spot in front of Ecole Militaire with a view of the Eiffel Tower. Fireworks on New Year's Eve are normally reserved for the Arc de Triomphe, but in 2014, they were also scheduled to be launched from the base of the Eiffel Tower.

When the display was over, the crowd seemed to be in an abnormal hurry to leave the area. Many of them ran to the Metro station. Following the crowd, we, too, boarded the train and fled without understanding the reason for the frenzy.

It was just above freezing as I sat at an outside table at Les Deux Magots the next morning. The overhead heater and my café au lait kept me warm enough as I read that day's *Le Parisien* and watched people pass by. The headline in the paper read, "Sea of people invades Champs-Élysées for New Year's Eve." The article mentioned that a seventeen-year-old was killed in a drunken fight during the celebrations near the Eiffel Tower. "On New Year's Eve," I thought, "while we were celebrating the birth of a new year, this young boy's life ended abruptly."

Although the inside of the café was nearly full, I was the only person to brave the cold on the patio.

"Sit anywhere over there," my waiter ordered a young woman, who took one of the tables on the other end of the patio. She appeared to be about thirty, too thin, wearing a plaid sweater, striped pants, and a black beret tilted to the left. Her clothing was a bit worn as was the large purse over her shoulder. The woman reminded me of June Miller, the close friend of the famous French author Anaïs Nin in the 1930s, from the movie *Henry & June.* When the waiter went back inside the café, the woman moved to the table next to mine and immediately lit a cigarette.

"Bon appétit," she offered as I ate my croissant, now smelling like smoke.

"Merci."

"I see that there are a lot of birds in the air."

Paris isn't really a place where the French will grab a table next to you just to strike up a conversation, but that woman was an exception. Since I had been in Paris for three weeks and had seen birds every day since my arrival, visual confirmation of our feathered friends seemed unnecessary.

Thinking that she might be from some birdless area of the country, I asked, "Where are you from?"

"Bordeaux. It's quite warm, and there's a beach there as well. Do you smoke?"

Having inhaled her cigarette smoke for a few minutes, I wanted to tell her I had just started smoking that morning but instead replied with a more polite "No, I don't smoke."

"Oh, that's too bad. I wish I'd known. I wouldn't have lit this cigarette." She continued to exhale in my direction. "And where are you from?"

"Florida. I'm here writing a book."

"Really? I'm writing a book too."

"What do you write about?" I asked.

"It's my diary. But I never show it to anyone." She quickly changed the subject. "Hey, look at the little bird under your table."

She sounded surprised that here was yet another winged creature of Paris. Quickly, she reached into her bag and threw a handful of bread pieces on the ground, attracting every bird within a block to the area previously occupied by my feet.

Déjà Vu

Attempting to distract her, I showed her the photograph on the front page of the newspaper. She took it out of my hands.

I waited patiently for her to look at the picture and return the paper. Instead, she sat smoking, reading every article until tears streamed down her face.

"Did you read this article about the seventeen-year-old who was killed? Who was he? Why did he get killed?"

She sobbed uncontrollably. Slowly, she closed the paper and returned it to me. "The poor guy."

Clearly overcome with emotion, she walked out to the side of the road to regain her composure.

My waiter, who had seen none of the incident, came outside and asked, "Where did she go?"

"She went out to the street to smoke."

He leaned toward me and in a quiet voice said, "She is bizarre, no?"

Evidently, she was one of his regulars.

"We are all bizarre in one way or another," I replied.

"Absolutely, monsieur. Absolutely."

Taking advantage of the momentary distraction, I left the 1930s and the café in favor of going to Shakespeare and Company for the day's writing.

I sat upstairs at the bookstore, writing the chapter that describes the terror of 1979, the time when terrorists blew up the Jewish restaurant on Rue de Médicis. Little did I know that even as I wrote those words, tragedy would strike the Jews of Paris again. One week later, Islamic terrorists held all the shoppers in a Jewish supermarket hostage,

killing four of them. The same week, others from the same terrorist group killed twelve cartoonists on the staff of *Charlie Hebdo*, a satirical newspaper. Thirty-six years had passed, and history repeated itself.

If the goal of the terrorists was to strike fear into the hearts of the citizens, then once again, it backfired. Later in the week, 1.8 million people took part in an antiterrorism march across the city—the largest gathering in the history of the republic. People of every race and religion marched arm in arm to protest this scar on their beloved Paris. As for me, it was time to return home.

There's a feeling that overwhelms me on the day before my departure from Paris. I find myself wanting to sit on a bench, close my eyes, and breathe her essence, hear every sound, and memorize the smell of every boulangerie. These are the souvenirs that I take with me. The French word "souvenir" translates in English as "to remember." But no amount of plastic Eiffel Towers, scarves imprinted with the word *Paris*, or postcards can take the place of the sights, sounds, and smells of being there. On this trip, my most cherished souvenir was the solidarity the Parisians displayed in the face of the latest tragedy. Paris was strong, and she would not let the terrorists win.

Freedom

EXPLORING FREEDOM - 2016

It was a sunny day in May, and Air France flight 1381 from London landed at Charles de Gaulle airport at 9 a.m., right on time. The line at passport control was more than an hour long but still faster than had I taken the Eurostar train, since the French rail service was on strike when I arrived. While the ride into the city was uneventful, the Uber driver hinted that a protest was planned over the 15 percent pay cut to be imposed on all Uber drivers. But that would be a matter for another day. This trip would end at Rue du Faubourg Montmartre for steak frites.

Thirty-nine years after my previous visit to Le Bouillon Chartier, I returned to see if this 150-year-old restaurant had succumbed to the new trends or if it was even still in business. It was 11:30 a.m., and the waiters stood outside, mentally preparing for the day, discussing the specials, and smoking cigarettes.

Once the staff filed inside, the head waiter seated me with three people from France—a young couple from Amiens and their cousin from Paris. The waiter explained that at Le Bouillon Chartier, strangers were seated together. I thought of the time when Mom, Dad, and I were seated next to the elderly Frenchman. Almost half a century later, I was the senior joining three others in the same restaurant. Our orders were taken then recorded on the paper tablecloth. My French tablemates ordered a carafe of wine for the table, telling me not to bother ordering wine on my own as it would be cheaper this way. Our bread basket was filled by combining leftover bread from two departing tables.

I explained that the drawers on the wall were used in the past by patrons storing their cloth napkins. In the end, save for the paper napkins, traditions had been passed on to the next generation, and nothing noticeable had changed.

My new friends at the table said, "The Americans don't come to Paris much anymore. They are afraid. Afraid of the terrorism, of the refugees. But look at us. No one will stop us from living our lives the way we always have. Without our freedom, we have nothing."

I wanted to learn more about this "freedom" of which the Parisians often spoke. With that in mind, I returned late in the fall and visited some of the locals to better under-stand their lives in the city. My first stop was Montmartre to visit Marie Noell, who had previously painted a sketch of my wife and me.

Very little about Montmartre has changed over the centuries. The Abbey de Montmartre was destroyed during the French Revolution, and all traces of the Commune of Paris, the heart of the civil war in the 1870s, have disappeared. But much still remains.

The Musée du Vieux Montmartre, located in a seventeenth-century home, lets us relive the times of Renoir, Van Gogh, and other "local" artists. And since 1635, the Place du Tertre has been hosting artists, some hoping to paint the next masterpiece.

Over coffee, I spoke with Marie Noell, a longtime painter in the square. Wisps of gray hair peeking out from underneath her thick woolen hat and lying on her weathered brow gave the only indication that this woman was likely in her sixties. As she unzipped her down jacket and sat, I could see a down vest and at least three more layers of thick shirts underneath, protecting her from the winter weather in the artist's square. Marie looked tired but was passionate about her work. Her face lit up when I asked her to share her story.

"Marie, how did you become a painter at Place du Tertre?"

"When I started forty years ago, it was a tournament. Then two or three years later, there were regulations that you had to spend time in a maison des artistes. Those who worked there had an opportunity to be placed in a spot. Because when you're accepted, it's still hard to get a place. They accept two artists for each place. There were three hundred placements and five hundred artists. And now there are fewer placements, and our spaces are only one meter square, which is too small. We are asking for more space."

I asked Marie if things had changed over her forty years in the square.

"It used to be that there was a waiting list, and when a vacancy arose, it was given to the one who had been waiting the longest. But as of four years ago, there's a contest. Now after two years of competing in the contest, you might get your place. So now we have better artists."

"What time of year is the best for the artists?" I asked.

"You're here in the winter, but it's not the same in the summer. In the summer, there are tables for the cafés taking up part of the terrace in the middle of the square. Right now, you can pick your spot. But from April until the first of November, there are café tables taking up about half of the space. So there are fewer painters. We take our vacation when there isn't much work. January is a good time for vacation, as there are few tourists."

It sounded like a tough life to me, and I asked if it was really worth it. "Today, you're wearing four or five layers of clothing just to stay warm. Why do you do it?"

"I like this profession primarily because I'm free. And with the new way of selecting artists, it works well for all of us. It's the liberty. There's no intermediary. I have direct contact with my customers, and the customers change all the time and come from everywhere. The painters, unfortunately, they paint the same subject many times, but that's the way it is."

Just then, an artist armed with black pencils and canvas came to our table, inviting us to have our pictures drawn while we continued our conversation. Marie quickly sent him away.

"These artists, you see them walking around, they are unauthorized and very bad. They couldn't get a space in the square, so they just walk around hoping to trick a tourist into thinking they really know their craft. And most of these galleries sell paintings made in China."

I was curious about silk screening. "Do any of these artists use silk screening to make many copies of a painting quickly?"

"Here, normally, it is forbidden. We are required to perform our work here in our place."

We finished our coffee with a discussion of her grandchildren, then she returned to her spot in the square, while I explored the nearby Square Suzanne Buisson.

In this square was a small park with a fountain containing a statue of none other than Saint Denis holding his own head. He likely had just washed the blood off of it before, as legend has it, he continued his famous headless journey down the hill.

The following day, the wind was blowing strong on the banks of the Seine, and the riverside booksellers were more interested in conversation than selling books. Along Quai Voltaire, leaves from nearby trees fell onto the books as if to cover them for the upcoming winter. Each of the more than two hundred vendors sells books out of their

mandated pine-green boxes, each not more than two meters wide. The bouquinistes are required to be open at least four days a week, and souvenirs cannot make up more than 25 percent of their sales. Yet the word I heard most often when they described their profession was "freedom."

My first encounter, not far from Musée D'Orsay, was with a bouquiniste who offered me only his first name, Henri. He put his book down to give me his full attention.

"It's not that there are fewer people who want to read, but there aren't as many book collectors as there were before," Henri explained. "Things are very different now. It used to be very easy to succeed as a bouquiniste, but now that the socialists have taken over, things are different. Many people no longer want a high-quality book. They just want something for three or four euros that they can read and leave at the hotel before they move on to another city."

He showed me a copy of a book in English called *Little Folks*.

"Look at this. Twenty-seven euros. What a fantastic deal! I found three of them, but nobody wants to buy them."

The book, written in 1904, looked to be in perfect condition. Henri pointed at miniatures of the Eiffel Tower. "But now people just want to buy this junk."

Upon reflection, Henri said, "I became a bookseller in 1991, working for someone else, and then ten years later, I got my own spot. Even now, there's nothing like it."

"Chapter seven. That's the best chapter. Look," Jean-Pierre Mathias told a customer considering a purchase of one of his books on philosophy. I asked Jean-Pierre if I could have a moment of his time to learn more about his profession. We sat down on a bench, and he ran to one of his boxes and pulled out a magazine article about the bouquinistes. Bouncing back and forth between me and his customers, Jean-Pierre was full of energy. He'd been doing this for twenty-five years and was known as "The Philosopher" or "Columbo" by his peers.

"I have a very small apartment in Paris, but most of it is taken up by my wife's piano. Our children take after their mother, and thus I am sending both of them to Juilliard."

While Jean-Pierre helped someone interested in a book on Existentialism, I came across a quote from a previous interview with him.

"It's not just buyers or sellers who appear at this bench. Sometimes, the hopeless or depressed join me here. I try to boost their morale, occasionally with good results. This bench gives people friendly help!"

Seated next to me, he pulled out a magazine article, and the first thing I noticed was a photo of him reading a book on the same bench where the two of us sat.

Jean-Pierre said he sells more souvenirs now than when he started. His excitement level reached a peak when a prospective customer came by looking for texts written by a particular philosopher. I left Jean-Pierre to focus on his customer and walked a bit farther to the next group of bouquinistes.

I met Marie-Christine Thieblemont along the Quai des Grands Augustins, where she specialized in books on the subject of fine art. Looking at me over her reading glasses, book in hand, she told me that after a decade of working for the historic Parisian art auction house Drouot, she became a bouquiniste. Even after working for more than twenty-five years on the banks of the Seine, Marie-Christine said she still enjoys working seven days a week.

I felt her passion as she described her latest offerings to the regular customers who drove by. Over the years, Marie-Christine has become a celebrity in her own right, and numerous magazine articles have been written about her and her life as a quintessential bouquiniste. In *Le Bonbon Rive Gauche,* she espoused the freedom of her profession.

"What is extraordinary to me is that as a bouquiniste, I can read all day. While raising five children, I never had time to read. Now I am recovering that time, with pleasure."

Why does she sell only books on art and sculpture?

Marie-Christine told me, "I have people who browse for an hour. Sometimes they buy, sometimes not. But because we share the same passion, the conversations are very interesting. Here, you are on the riverside of the intellectuals."

She smiled and returned to reading her book.

DEATH IN PARIS

It is fall, and the weather is cooler, and so are the locals. The Frenchman I met in a café explained.

"In August, it is hot, and there is plenty of sun. We are excited to leave Paris and head to the beach for the month. We return happy, energized, and ready for anything. The sun still warms the day and illuminates the evenings. But in mid-October, the sun begins to hide, and the weather becomes cool and windy. By the beginning of November, we Parisians, as if part of an ancient ritual and mourning the death of the sun, dress in black."

He pointed at my clothing and continued. "We would never wear a ski jacket in the city. Parisians aren't happy that winter is coming. You, monsieur, are wearing a dark-blue ski jacket and are smiling. Surely you are not from Paris. Parisians remain in mourning until December, when the holidays are near. Christmas and New Year's give us hope, and our smiles return."

With all this talk of death and cold weather, it was a good time to head underground. Along with about one hundred people dressed in black, I, dressed in somewhat brighter colors, waited ninety minutes in line outside Denfert-Rochereau to see the catacombs.

After hundreds of steps and roughly one-half mile of walking through dimly lit corridors under the streets of Paris, I followed the guide and entered the catacombs of Paris.

"Stop—This is the Kingdom of the Dead," warned the sign above my head.

Upon entering, I was greeted by piles of bones neatly stacked six feet high. A row of skulls on top looked right at me. For over half an hour, I walked through room after cold, damp room of the bones of dead Parisians. The eerie silence was broken only by the sounds of the footsteps of us mortals passing by those less fortunate. A path marked the way forward, but the many dark corridors on each side contained a total of six million skeletons—roughly three times the number of live Parisians who roamed the city above me.

The revolution was gruesome, and I remembered Heidi telling me that over forty thousand people died from the guillotine. But the number of people underground was in the millions. I asked the guide where these bones came from.

She explained, "In 1786, bones were moved from the Cimetière des Innocents into underground quarries where stone had been mined for buildings such as Notre Dame Paris. The cemeteries of Paris were overcrowded and had become a health risk, with many bodies left to rot above ground in cemetery buildings. To make matters worse, some of these buildings were near Le Marais, the large food market. Cemeteries were emptied and bodies transferred into the catacombs. The relocation was done under the cover of night because there had been concern that the religious population would object to seeing their departed loved ones dismembered and neatly piled underground. This process continued for many years, with bones from hundreds of graveyards having been moved here to the catacombs."

There's a lot more to the Paris underground than just piles of bones. Directly under the bustling city, a secret world of artwork, candlelit theaters, canals, and reservoirs exists in the abandoned mines. Only cataphiles, members of a secret "society," know the details of this city hidden below.

Since the twelfth century, areas outside the city were mined for limestone underground. As the city expanded, buildings were unknowingly constructed directly above these unmapped quarries. The best estimates are that there are almost two hundred miles of quarry tunnels under Paris, their existence remaining mostly unknown to those living directly above.

Near the end of the 1700s, several people and their homes descended into a collapsed tunnel in the area now known as Denfert Rochereau. After additional buildings disappeared into the underground, King Louis XVI directed a team to map these dangerous caverns, shoring up those most in need. So many caverns were discovered that the underground is sometimes referred to as "The Gruyère de Paris" because the underground is full of holes, just like

Swiss cheese. In fact, some say that roughly 20 percent of the city and its suburbs are in areas at risk of collapse. And not all the tunnels have yet been discovered and mapped.

In 1961, an entire neighborhood of a Parisian suburb fell into the ground when a chalk quarry gave way. With more than twenty dead, Parisians were once again reminded of the fragile landscape below. As recently as 2015, a sinkhole developed in the 19th arrondissement.

Not wanting to become one of the skeletons forever entombed in these caves during the next collapse, I emerged from the catacombs and took a deep breath of cool autumn air on terra firma.

Catacombs

UP IN SMOKE - 2019

"Notre Dame on fire," read the message on my phone. Sitting at the dinner table at a friend's house in northern Italy, I hid my tears as the live video unfolded before my eyes. Soon, the spire came crashing down through the cathedral's roof. Thoughts of my time at Notre Dame raced through my head. Meeting Heidi outside the front doors, our walks through the rose garden out back, and the times I was fortunate enough to hear the organ reverberating throughout the structure. Gone. Possibly forever.

I had to get to Paris. I had to see her.

It took me a few months, but on a hot summer day, I made it back and went straight to Notre Dame. She looked empty and hollow without her roof or the statues of the apostles looking up toward the spire. I felt as if I was at a closed-coffin funeral of a close friend. Covered in melted scaffolding and isolated by corrugated metal fencing, the cathedral was unreachable, as if she were a broken relic from another time. Taking time to study the structure from outside Shakespeare and Company, I could see Notre Dame truly was in ruins. After surviving countless wars, revolutions, and uprisings, she was likely done in by a cigarette butt left behind by workers on the wooden roof, who ironically had been restoring the original steeple. Then, a new employee misunderstood the location of the warning given by the fire alarm system, causing a long delay in the call to the fire department, thus sealing the cathedral's fate.

During the fire, molten lead used centuries ago to seal the roof came down on unprotected firemen, not unlike Quasimodo in the Victor Hugo classic *The Hunchback of Notre Dame*. It took days to completely extinguish the embers.

The scaffolding from the original restoration work was now just six tons of twisted metal hanging precariously over the top of the structure. If this scaffolding were to fall, the rest of the building would collapse around it. The army had been called in to study the problem and devise a way to remove the metal without causing further damage to the cathedral.

A leading expert at the National Institute of Health said in a French newspaper, "We have to realize that the four hundred tons of lead that were spread corresponds to four times the lead emissions in the whole of France for a year. The cathedral has now become filled with toxic waste."

Dazed, I sat on a bench and looked over the fence at what remained of the cathedral. Seeing her as a shell of her prior self, I was finally struck by the loss.

A Parisian seated next to me saw the tears streaming down my face and shared her feelings about the fire. "The high fencing is there to protect us from cleanup work being done by people in Chernobyl suits because of the poisonous lead everywhere. The lead is causing quite a problem, with local restaurants being forced to close due to contamination, allowed to reopen, and then closed again. Children from schools in this area have been measured with high levels of lead in their bodies. Yes, the fire was terrible. But we will persevere, and our Notre Dame will return. Of this, I am sure."

Just then, an English-speaking tour guide followed by about fifteen tourists stopped next to the fountain in front of my bench.

"This green fountain was installed by an Englishman in 1872 and is one of roughly twelve hundred drinking fountains across the city. Some even have the option of sparkling water. They contain the purest, best-tasting water around, so be sure to fill up your bottles here."

Declining to take her advice, I took a walk in search of a cold lead-free beverage far away from Notre Dame.

In just a few minutes, I had arrived at the beaches of Paris. While it's true that Paris is hundreds of miles from the ocean, every summer since 2002, the city of Paris has transformed the banks of the Seine river, which meanders through the city, into a tropical paradise. Looking down from Pont Neuf, I saw hundreds of lounge chairs, umbrellas, and picnic tables on newly installed grass set up for the summer. Parisians in bathing suits relaxed as if they were actually on the beach.

The riverbanks were much quieter than in years past. The lower road that runs along the Seine was closed to vehicles, providing me and others a place to stroll at our own pace. This modern transformation of the city center, according to the City of Paris, reduces pollution and provides a respite for locals who can't afford to head to the coast for a seaside vacation—or just don't have the freedom to. Tons of sand were brought in and poured onto the sidewalks lining the river. There were swimming pools as well as volleyball courts, misting fountains, and miniature golf for the children. Adults played pétanque and practiced tai chi. I briefly considered trying the zip line, set up for the more adventurous beachgoers. Paris was undergoing yet another renaissance, and the evidence was everywhere.

LET THEM EAT BREAD - 2021

At nearly sixty-five, I had come to realize that dreams change when reality intervenes. After spending more than a year living in Venice in 2005, my wife and I decided to retire in 2018 and move to Liguria in northern Italy, five hours from Venice and eight hours from Paris. Financially, it made more sense, as the cost of living is far less than in Paris. From our new location, we enjoy everything Italy, France, and the rest of Europe have to offer. We still visit Paris frequently but only as tourists.

We live an hour from Nice, giving us an opportunity to make a monthly shopping run to purchase French cheeses, cider, meats, butter, and cream. But nothing compares to the bread and pastries in Paris.

In 2020 and most of 2021, the coronavirus pandemic kept us at home in Italy. But in mid-2021, travel restrictions had eased enough for me to take a high-speed train from Nice to Paris. To continue living in Italy, I needed a set of my fingerprints produced by an authorized agency to give to the Italian government. A tiny one-person firm in Paris that primarily provided fingerprints for pilots was more easily accessible to me than the firms in Rome. So, I made a quick trip to Paris. For five and a half hours, the train traversed a countryside teeming with castles on the way to the Paris Gare de Lyon station. My first stop was at Place Maubert. After picking up a bottle of fifteen-year-old Calvados for the house, I walked straight to my favorite place for butter croissants, La Maison d'Isabelle. Their croissants were heavenly but not quite as good as the memories of those from our neighborhood boulangerie where I bought pastries every morning for Heidi and me.

"2018 First Prize of Paris and Île-de-France Butter Croissant." The banner hanging above La Maison d'Isabelle proudly announced the news. Along with having won the award for the best butter croissants in the Paris region, they also won for the best apple tart. I'd known for some time that this tiny boulangerie was special, and now it had been confirmed by the Syndicat des Boulangers du Grand Paris.

The Parisians take their bread and pastries seriously. Each year for over thirty years, roughly 250 boulangeries have submitted their best croissants for judging. These delicious rolls are evaluated using specific criteria for appearance as well as texture and taste. A quality croissant will have a shine to the perfectly formed exterior, and the aroma of high-quality butter and yeast should permeate the air when it's pulled apart.

My croissants were still warm when I sat in the square to enjoy them. No jelly or additional butter is necessary

when the steam escapes as the pastry is opened. It was easy to understand why La Maison d'Isabelle won its award.

The ubiquitous baguette is held in even greater esteem. In fact, the French government has requested that the baguette be added to the UNESCO list of world heritage sites. To be permitted in the competition for the best baguette in Paris, the loaf must be between 50 and 55 centimeters long, weigh between 250 and 270 grams, and have no more than 18 grams of salt per kilogram of flour. Some years, over half of the entries are rejected without ever being judged, due to these strict criteria. These rejected loaves don't go to waste, however. They're donated to charity to help feed the homeless.

The morning paper had mentioned that the baguette judging was being held that afternoon in a huge tent directly in front of Notre Dame. Walking toward the courtyard, I found the rich smell of fermented yeast was already in the air. Nothing, no scent the perfume makers on the right bank could invent, can possibly compete with the scent of hot baguettes fresh out of the oven. I stood watching the jury members slicing the numbered baguettes, not knowing the bakers of each glorious loaf.

The contestants aren't judged solely by a smug group of bakers and journalists. Half of the tasters are Parisian residents picked by lottery. The winning baker is awarded not only the monetary prize of four thousand euros but also has the honor of supplying bread to the president of France for a year.

Nowhere is there a better example of successful integration of immigrants than in the list of winners. In the nine years from 2013 to 2021, five of the winners had Tunisian origins and one was from Senegal. Only three bakers had French roots.

Djibril Bodian, the baker of Senegal origin, recalled, "When I became a baker twenty-two years ago, no one thought that a baguette could bring you to the Elysée Palace!"

For those of us not on the jury, products from the competing bakeries were for sale. I purchased a pain au raisin overflowing with pastry cream and arrived at my fingerprinting appointment satisfied to be just a member of the general public.

With my fingerprints processed and my Paris shopping completed, the next day, I grabbed a few of Bodian's baguettes at his bakery, Le Grenier à Pain, and made myself a ham, cheese, and butter sandwich for the train ride back to Nice. Watching the scenery out the train window, I imagined French President Emmanuel Macron having the same meal in his palace.

BASTILLE DAY - 2022

July 14, 2022, fell upon a very different Paris than it had in years gone by. For almost three years, the city had been in various versions of lockdown or slowdown due to the pandemic. It was sad to see that some of the old boulangeries, restaurants, and for better or worse, even some of the Starbucks coffee shops had disappeared. Many, however, had been replaced with various ethnic restaurants. As I walked down Rue Mouffetard, the smell of Mexican chipotle and barbacoa filled the air at the new Bocamexa, and the scent of curry wafted from the Japanese Papillon across the street.

As the city rebounds, a new type of renaissance is taking hold. Scooters and bicycles can be rented and returned on virtually every street. Car lanes in the city center are being partially replaced by lanes for these readily available modes of personal transportation. The old girl is becoming greener. Hydrogen and electric buses are slowly being rolled out. As the odor from exhaust fumes is reduced, the aroma from the bakeries becomes more apparent. Preparations are underway for the Summer 2024 Olympics.

More space is being made available for outside dining. The huge underground mall at Les Halles has gone through a transformational renovation into a modern mall complete with gym, billiards, swimming pool, and a new movie theater. Mayor Hidalgo wants to add almost two hundred kilometers of bicycle lanes by 2026.

After the struggle of the last few years, Paris could have declined as many cities have done. But its leaders have risen to the challenges and used the slowdown as a time to implement changes, preparing her for the future. Even Notre Dame is being rebuilt better and stronger than ever. The scaffolding melted from the fire has been carefully removed and replaced. Special joists were put in place to stabilize the cathedral during reconstruction. Limestone may be mined from the depths of the catacombs to replace the stones lost in the fire, using pieces from the same quarry to match the weight and density of the originals mined 750 years ago. In this way, the six million skeletons from days gone by can give new life to Notre Dame. Although the work may be too complex to be completed within the five-year targeted timeframe, the cathedral will return, to the delight of Parisians and tourists alike.

Debbie and I were in Paris to share our favorite spots with friends Bill and Lisa, who flew from Ireland to join us there. This was also a chance for me to revisit some of my old haunts and experience some of the Parisian rebirth.

Our first stop was La Samaritaine, an art nouveau department store near Pont Neuf, which opened in 1869. It closed in 2005 and had just reopened. Like a jewel, cleaned and polished to its original splendor, it featured glass tile floors, iron staircases, and floral frescoes true to the style of the late 1800s.

I made sure our friends saw the Galeries Lafayette, the second-most-visited monument in Paris after the Eiffel Tower. Built in the 1890s, this department store was then known as a "luxury bazaar." Looking up upon entering the store, we were bathed in the golden light of the forty-three-meter-high glass dome above the atrium, which spotlights the giant staircase inspired by the Garnier Opera House. Everything in the store appeared to have been covered in gold. It looked much more like a palace than an indoor shopping mall. The views of the Eiffel Tower and Montmartre from the rooftop left our friends in awe.

We then visited the restyled Gare d'Orsay, turned into a museum in 1986. Entering the Musée d'Orsay gave me the feeling of being in the old majestic train station, with a high glass panel ceiling, arched windows, and an old gold clock hanging on the glass wall. Now, instead of trains, it holds the largest collection of Impressionist and Postimpressionist art in the world. Monet, Manet, Renoir, Cézanne, and Van Gogh are among the masters represented there. Full of natural light, the repurposed Gare d'Orsay still gave us the opportunity for a voyage. But instead of cold steel rails, we traveled via the eyes of the greatest artists to distant lands and forgotten times. Gazing at Claude Monet's *The Rocks at Belle-Ile, The Wild Coast* transported me back to 1979 and my time with a French family in Brittany.

Leaving the museum, Lisa asked, "Can we have a picnic in that big field under the Eiffel Tower?"

Since it was a very hot summer day, we agreed to meet up again at nine o'clock in the evening, just before sunset. Debbie and I would supply the food, and our friends planned to bring wine and a blanket from their hotel for us to sit on in the park.

Many stores are closed on Bastille Day. In fact, one of the few places I could find that sold meat and cheese was a gas station near Place d'Italie. I had to laugh. Here I was in the culinary capital of the world, preparing for a picnic with gas station salami and gas station cheese, all in plastic packaging. A baguette, a squeeze bottle of organic mayonnaise, and a corkscrew completed my treasure hunt.

The Champ de Mars, the rectangular field of grass where we were to meet, offered an unobstructed view of the Eiffel Tower and the setting sun. My perception of this park had always been one of drunks, pigeons, and garbage, so I had no reason to visit. As we unwrapped the bed runner borrowed from our friends' hotel, I saw a different picture. Many couples brought picnic baskets full of gourmet meals and charcuterie served on small tables with glasses of wine. Children ran in the open space, some blowing bubbles while others napped in their strollers. Even the hawkers selling battery-operated Eiffel Towers did so unobtrusively.

As the sun set and the sky filled the spaces between the clouds with a subdued orange, the tower dazzled us with sparkling white lights. We were sharing this moment in this field with people from around the world. Good friends, a great location, and a bottle of wine were more important than the culinary deficiencies in our picnic. I couldn't believe it had taken me more than forty years to discover the beauty of Champ de Mars. Paris is still teaching me, just as she did the first time I arrived.

The next evening found the four of us outside the Panthéon, looking out over Luxembourg Gardens while dining at Le Comptoir du Panthéon. With the Eiffel Tower sparkling in the distance, our friend Lisa said to me, "It's my last night in Paris, and I haven't had a single crepe. Can you take me to that crepe restaurant across the street?"

Lisa and I ran across Rue Soufflot, leaving Bill and Debbie to finish their drinks. Service was slow, and by the time we finished our crepes, we were past ready to return to Debbie and Bill, still visible at the restaurant across the street. But our check hadn't arrived at the table.

"Lisa, I have an idea. Wait here, and I'll go pay."

I got up and found the manager. My voice hushed, I whispered, "I need your help. That woman I'm sitting with isn't my wife. And do you see that woman across the street with that man? That's my wife. I've got to get out of here quick!"

"I understand completely," the manager responded. "Here's your change. Now go!"

As I ran out the door with Lisa, we could hear the manager say, "Be careful!"

Back across the street with Debbie and Bill, we laughed while explaining our exit strategy to the waiter there at Le Comptoir du Panthéon.

"You know, the owner of this restaurant also owns the crèperie. Every night after closing, we all get together, have drinks, and share the stories of the day. I'm sure I'll hear this one tonight!"

The following day, our friends returned home, leaving Debbie and me to enjoy the city on our own. We have a tradition of visiting Place du Tertre on Montmartre every five years or so to have another picture drawn of the two of us. This year, the café in the center of the square expanded, pushing out more of the artists. It was as if having a few token painters would somehow legitimize this historic location. With 2022 being our twenty-fifth wedding anniversary, we chose our artist carefully, looking at samples of their work. When our session was over and the artist showed us the final drawing, I said, "Debbie, he did a great job with you, but why do I look so old?"

Walking downhill with our latest artwork, we stopped for lunch at Koff World Famous Burgers along the quiet Rue de Vieuville just down the street from Le Mur des Je t'Aime, an artist's wall with a mural of the phrase "I love you" written in over three hundred languages.

As we ate our burgers and fries in this idyllic location, a lady directly across the street yelled, "Help! He stole my purse!"

Two men were running away when two hikers with backpacks knocked them to the pavement and sat on top of them. Thinking that this could escalate quickly, we stood up and were about to run for safety when, almost in unison, the two men reached into their backpacks, handcuffed the robbers, and radioed for backup. These two undercover policemen had caught the thieves in under ten seconds before returning the purse to the tourist across the street. Feeling safer, we went back to our business of enjoying burgers and fries before heading to the Seine for a relaxing walk to Notre Dame.

Along the right bank, the beaches of Paris were going strong, with people in bathing suits lying in lounge chairs while others visited the temporary bars and cafés set up along the riverside. At street level, throngs of tourists packed the sidewalks, while Debbie and I shared the left bank sidewalk along the river with only an occasional tourist or two. We sat in a shady spot along the water's edge to enjoy the music of a bluegrass band with Notre Dame directly behind us, construction walls obstructing the view. In the center of the capital of France, in a city of over two million people, there we were on our anniversary, having essentially a private concert by an excellent band. Who knew, maybe they were practicing for a concert that night. I found myself adding money to their basket after every song. After forty-five years, Paris was still surprising me.

On the last night of our anniversary trip, we wondered whether we should dine at one of the many fancy restaurants or at a local bistro. We decided to celebrate in the manner in which we'd started—with bread, cheese, and a Tarte Normande from the patisserie on Île-Saint-Louis, followed by a late-night crepe in the Latin Quarter.

Paris for Life

FALL 2022

Our Ligurian hillside town in northern Italy has just 1,300 residents, with strong contingents of French, Germans, British, Australians, and New Zealanders. One of our good friends is Kerrie, a twentysomething resident who models in Milan and hails from Auckland. She came to me with a request.

"Barry, I'm dating an opera singer in Nice, but I don't speak French, and his English isn't very good. Could you teach me French?"

We arranged to meet twice a week to resolve any issues she might be having with her self-taught French curriculum. After only a few weeks, she had progressed so rapidly that my help was no longer needed. At the end of our last lesson, I reached into my backpack and gave her my forty-five-year-old copy of *Le Petit Nicolas* that Heidi had given me during my early days in Paris.

"This is for you. It served me well in practicing French. Now it's your turn. After all, if you're going to be in France, you need to truly understand the language." Heidi's voice echoed inside my head as I heard myself say those words.

Kerrie tucked the book inside her purse and took the next train to Nice. Listening to Kerrie speak about her French romance took me back to the Parisian romance I almost had years ago. A few days later, I found myself making a trip of my own to Paris.

Upon arriving, I discovered that most Metro lines were closed due to a strike over pensions. The buses were delayed and overflowing with commuters. From Notre Dame, I took a long walk up Boulevard Saint-Michel to the Luxembourg station. Hungry and thirsty, I hoped to find the nephew of my old Greek friend making crepes, but the crepe stand had disappeared. There was no trace of the place where I had enjoyed this perfectly prepared French delicacy for more than four decades. Only a faded square on the concrete slab outside Le Petit Journal remained where his kiosk once stood.

I waited on that concrete square as if somehow expecting to be transported back in time to that first egg-and-cheese crepe while watching my parents enjoy theirs. I thought of the time when my children, too, tried them for the first time. The smile on my daughter Amber's face as the butter oozed down her arm came back to me. A check with the owner of the jazz club confirmed my suspicions.

The nephew had retired and moved to England just as his uncle had done years ago. The kiosk was gone forever.

C'est la vie. I was fortunate to have enjoyed it for almost half a century. A new crepe stand had just opened around the corner, operated by a vibrant pair of Parisians no more than thirty years old. New flavors of crepes abounded, including some filled with ice cream. After choosing my old standard, egg and cheese, I turned to go to Luxembourg Gardens and tripped over a scooter left in the middle of the sidewalk. These electric scooters were everywhere, as Parisians commute using any means possible. Normally operated by younger people who likely haven't yet experienced broken bones, even locals in suits had taken to riding them due to the Metro strike. These rented scooters whizzed by pedestrians, and the riders frequently used the bus lanes. It could be a great way to reach your final destination more quickly.

In Luxembourg Gardens, the statue of Queen Marie de Médicis looked out over the grounds. Four hundred years had passed since she had enjoyed the park. Yet even today, with scooters, electric bicycles, and tablet book readers, people continue to find new ways to enjoy the queen's flowering work of art. My walk continued to my old school, the Alliance Française.

"I am possibly a little late for class. It was supposed to start on the fourteenth of February 1979," I joked with the receptionist. "Madame Ankaoua will be upset."

L'Alliance Française, Paris

Turning toward the grand staircase leading up to the classrooms, I remembered how we ran up the stairs each day, excited to learn. They were the same stairs where Adel got help with his classwork from Petra from Germany then walked away abruptly when another Iranian student arrived. I looked at that stairway and realized how much that building had changed my life forever.

The receptionist saw me gazing up the stairs, smiled, and said, "It's changed quite a bit since you were here, no? Feel free to take a look around."

True, the building had been modified. It was certainly larger. But at its heart, it was the same old school filled with the hopes and dreams of young men and women wanting to discover another culture, learn a new language, and change their lives.

A group of students arrived and rushed up the staircase toward their classrooms, and I stepped out of the way.

Retracing my old steps from the school to my old apartment, I walked through Luxembourg Gardens and watched the people play tennis on the same courts where Madame used to play. The chairs were full of people soaking up the sun, drawing, reading, enjoying each other and their surroundings. Children still chased the birds around the lake and launched their boats into the water with long sticks. Conversations in countless languages filled the air. Smiling, I took it all in, wondering what adventures awaited this new generation of dreamers hoping to experience Paris for life.

Epilogue

PARIS UPDATE - SPRING 2023

Sleeper trains, long absent in Europe, are making a comeback. Last night, I slept on a top bunk couchette in a shiny new air-conditioned train car from Nice to Paris. It was so nice to be able to arrive in downtown Paris at 7:30 a.m., ready to start the day with a croissant and café au lait in a nearby bar.

Parisians have tired of tripping over rental scooters. Last week, they voted 4-1 in favor of removing them from the city.

A few weeks before my arrival, tens of thousands of people rioted in the streets in the continuing unrest relating to pension reforms. The issue is still unresolved.

The new spire for Notre Dame, made from 150-year-old trees, has been delivered to Paris. It is entirely possible that the reconstruction project could be completed on time in 2024, with the cathedral open for Christmas of that year.

HEIDI - 2023

It's a cold and rainy day in May here in Paris. I'm almost sixty-six, sitting in Luxembourg Gardens like a teenager, reading and rereading a postcard, wondering what to think.

A week ago, I tried to find a photo of Heidi to use in this book. Although I thoroughly searched my archives at home, I found not a single photo of her. Like a ghost, she came into my life then vanished without a trace. But while flipping through old photos and mail I had saved from Paris, I found a folder labeled "Important Papers" with an envelope containing copies of my visa application forms. Stuck to one of them was a postcard from Heidi, which she must have sent to me from Switzerland during her military training in mid-1979. I had never seen this postcard before. Possibly in my haste, I stuffed it into the envelope, unseen until now, in 2023. My mind raced as I read her words.

Why had Heidi never shared her feelings about me? Was she waiting for me to respond favorably to what she wrote in the postcard, and when I didn't, she decided to return to Switzerland, leaving Paris for good? Had we both been afraid to tell each other how we felt?

It seemed that Paris had one final mystery up her sleeve. The postcard read:

Dear Sweetie:

It's the last day of military service, and I am very happy that we will see each other again soon. I hope that we are together before you receive this card. Happily, I have had a pile of work such that I could not always think of you; the distance would make it even more painful.

I love you.

See you soon,
Heidi

Postcard from Heidi, 1979

Bibliography

Digby Warde-ALDAM, "War and Pissoirs: How the Urinals of Paris helped beat the Nazis" (*The Guardian*, December 2, 2019)

Alain de BOTTON, *The Art of Travel* (Vintage Books, 2004)

Lindsey GALLOWAY, "Four Health-Conscious Cities Putting Pedestrians First" (BBC.COM, September 13, 2022)

Edwina HART, "How I Ended Up Sleeping in the World's Most Famous Bookstore" (*Lonely Planet*, June 17, 2020)

HOOG & Meyer, *Versailles: Complete Guide* (Editions d'Art, 1991)

Emily MONACO, "The perfect French Baguette" (BBC.COM, August 26, 2019)

Merle SEVERY, "France Celebrates Its Bicentennial" (*National Geographic*, July 1989)

Neil SHEA, "Under Paris" (*National Geographic*, February 2011)

Guy SILVA, *Avec Les Bouquinistes des Quais de Paris* (Le Castor Astral, 2000)

Tony SPAWFORTH, *Versailles: A Biography of a Palace* (St. Martin's Press, 2010)

--------, L'histoire de Rungis (rungisinternational.com, 2022)

--------, Clamart (*Le Figaro*, June 2, 1961)

--------, "L'encombrant héritage des sous-sols en gruyère de Paris" (*Le Figaro*, July 29, 2016)

--------, Le Bonbon Rive Gauche (September 2013)

--------, Paris Worldwide Numero 15 (2016)

Useful Addresses

Alliance Française
101 Boulevard Raspail
75006 Paris

Les Deux Magots
6 Place Saint-Germain des Prés
75006 Paris

Shakespeare and Company
37 Rue de la Bucherie
75005 Paris

Du Pain et Des Idées
34 rue Yves Toudic
75010 Paris

La Maison d'Isabelle
47 Ter Boulevard Saint Germain
75005 Paris

Le Bouillon-Chartier
7 Rue du Faubourg Montmartre
75009 Paris

Musée Marmottan Monet
2 rue Louis Boilly
75016 Paris

About the Author

Barry Frangipane doesn't write books—he simply puts pen to paper and lets his life (and sense of humor) spill onto the page. Born in New Jersey, USA, Barry became infected with wanderlust in his youth and has failed to find a cure ever since. He has traveled extensively, operated an exclusive European tour company, and eaten more crepes than he cares to mention. Most recently, he found himself captivated by Liguria, Italy, and is now retired there with his wife. Barry claims to know French, Italian, English, and the names of several other languages.

Barry and Debbie, circa 2020

Printed in the USA
CPSIA information can be obtained
at www.ICGtesting.com
JSHW080315031123
51396JS00001B/26